NATURAL ENVIRONMENT RESEARCH COUNCIL
INSTITUTE OF GEOLOGICAL SCIENCES

Geological Survey and Museum

BRITISH REGIONAL GEOLOGY

Scotland:
The Northern Highlands

THIRD EDITION

By

J. Phemister, M.A., D.Sc.

EDINBURGH
HER MAJESTY'S STATIONERY OFFICE
1960

The Institute of Geological Sciences
was formed by the
incorporation of the Geological Survey of Great Britain
and the Museum of Practical Geology
with Overseas Geological Surveys
and is a constituent body of the
Natural Environment Research Council

First published	-	-	-	-	-	1936
Third edition -	-	-	-	-	-	1960
Third impression (*with additional references*)	-	-	-	-	-	1965
Fifth impression	-	-	-	-	-	1970
Sixth impression	-	-	-	-	-	1974

SBN 11 880151 1

FOREWORD TO THE SECOND EDITION

The author wishes to acknowledge assistance received from colleagues on the Geological Survey, who have freely offered new information and helpful criticism. Dr. Pringle has rendered assistance on the palaeontological side. The published one-inch geological maps have provided the basis for almost all the maps in the text, but in Figs. 8 and 18 geological lines have been taken from maps which are still in manuscript. Fig. 9 has been redrawn from Plate XII in 'The Geology of Ben Wyvis' (*Mem. Geol. Survey*), 1912, and the sections in Figs. 7, 10, 14, 15, and 22 are reproduced from or based on sections in Geological Survey memoirs. The section, Fig. 3, is copied from B. N. Peach and J. Horne, 'Chapters on the Geology of Scotland' (Oxford University Press), 1930. The illustrations of Middle Old Red Sandstone fossils have been drawn by Mr. J. K. Allan from restorations by R. H. Traquair and Prof. D. M. S. Watson.

In preparing the second edition of this handbook the author has been indebted to Mr. V. A. Eyles, Dr. A. G. MacGregor and Mr. T. H. Whitehead for useful criticism and for information on the results of recent work in the West Highlands.

FOREWORD TO THE THIRD EDITION

During the years that have passed since the publication of the second edition of this volume, extensive and detailed research has been going on in the Northern Highlands, and in reprints (1952, 1954) attention was drawn to some of the work which was being published by extending the lists of references. In the present edition references to literature have been brought up to date and comments have been added in the text, but because the interpretation of much of the research on the metamorphic rocks is still a matter of controversy it has not been thought necessary, or indeed profitable, to discuss at the present time the various hypotheses which have been proposed. Readers interested in the evolution of ideas about the structure and metamorphism of the rocks of the Northern Highlands may consult the author's 'Summary of Recent Research on the pre-Tertiary Geology of the Northern Highlands' (*Trans. Geol. Soc. Glasgow*, vol. xxiii, 1958). In preparing the present edition the author has been greatly indebted to Dr. A. G. MacGregor for assistance.

An EXHIBIT illustrating the Geology and Scenery of the district described in this volume is set out on the First Gallery of the Museum of Practical Geology, Exhibition Road, South Kensington, London. S.W.7.

PREFACE TO THE SECOND EDITION

CONTENTS

		PAGE
I.	INTRODUCTION	1
	Physical Features: Scenery	1
	Summary of the Geology and Table of Formations	3
II.	LEWISIAN GNEISS	7
	Paragneiss of the Lewisian Complex	7
	Orthogneiss of the Lewisian Complex	9
	Later Intrusions	12
	Lewisian Inliers in the Moine Schists	12
	Foliation and Pre-Torridonian Movements	13
III.	MOINE SERIES	17
	The Moine Schists	17
	Tarskavaig Moine Rocks	26
	Pre-foliation Intrusions	26
	Granite-Schist Injection-Complexes	30
	Age of the Moine Series	35
IV.	TORRIDONIAN	41
V.	CAMBRIAN AND EARLY ORDOVICIAN	47
VI.	POST-CAMBRIAN INTRUSIONS IN ASSYNT	52
VII.	POST-CAMBRIAN THRUST-MOVEMENTS	55
VIII.	NEWER IGNEOUS ROCKS	60
	Loch Loyal Syenites	60
	Foliated Lamprophyre	61
	Ach'uaine Hybrid and Appinite Suite	61
	Granite—Granodiorite—Diorite	64
	Later Hypabyssal Intrusions	67
	Age Relations	68
IX.	OLD RED SANDSTONE	71
	Middle Old Red Sandstone	71
	Upper Old Red Sandstone	79
X.	CARBONIFEROUS	81
XI.	LATER MINOR INTRUSIONS	82
XII.	MESOZOIC AND TERTIARY	84
	Trias	84
	Jurassic	84
	Cretaceous	90
	Tertiary	90
XIII.	FAULTS	92
XIV.	PLEISTOCENE AND RECENT	94
	Glacial Period	94
	Raised Beaches	98
	Cave Deposits	99
XV.	MINERALS, etc.	101
	LIST OF GEOLOGICAL SURVEY PUBLICATIONS	103

Selected Bibliographies are appended to each of the Sections I-XV.

LIST OF ILLUSTRATIONS

FIGURES IN TEXT

PAGE

FIG. 1. Boundaries and physiography of the Northern Highlands 2

FIG. 2. Section across the northern mainland of Scotland 6

FIG. 3. Section across the Loch Maree belt of paragneiss 8

FIG. 4. Distribution of the Lewisian Gneiss 10

FIG. 5. Foliation of the Lewisian Gneiss and distribution of pre-Torridonian intrusions 14

FIG. 6. Distribution of the lithological groups of the Moine Schists .. 20

FIG. 7. Sections in the Moine Schists 22

FIG. 8. Geological map of southern Sleat, Skye; sections illustrating the occurrence of the Tarskavaig Moine Rocks 25

FIG. 9. Pre-foliation intrusions and contact-aureole at Càrn Chuinneag and Inchbae 29

FIG. 10. Sections illustrating the unconformity of Torridon Sandstone on Lewisian Gneiss 42

FIG. 11. Distribution of the groups of the Torridon Sandstone 43

FIG. 12. Section illustrating the unconformity of Cambrian strata on Torridon Sandstone and Lewisian Gneiss 47

FIG. 13. Vertical section of the Cambrian and Early Ordovician 48

FIG. 14. Sections across the post-Cambrian thrust-belt 58

FIG. 15. Sections across the post-Cambrian thrust-belt in Assynt 59

FIG. 16. ⎰Large pre-foliation intrusions in the Moine Series, injection-⎱ 62
and ⎱complexes, post-Cambrian intrusions in Assynt, and 'Newer⎰ and
FIG. 17. ⎱Igneous' rocks .. .. ⎰ 63

FIG. 18. The Strontian Granite 66

FIG. 19. The Old Red Sandstone of Caithness and Sutherland 72

FIG. 20. Section from Morven to Berriedale 73

FIG. 21. The Old Red Sandstone of Ross-shire and part of Inverness-shire .. 76

FIG. 22. Section from Strathpeffer to the Black Isle 77

FIG. 23. Middle Old Red Sandstone fishes 78

FIG. 24. Middle Old Red Sandstone fishes 79

FIG. 25. Trias and Lias of Wester Ross 85

FIG. 26. Mesozoic rocks of East Sutherland and the Cromarty area .. 86

FIG. 27. Glaciation of the Northern Highlands 95

PLATES

PLATE   I. Diorama illustrating the scenery and geological structure of the North-west Highlands. On the right Quinag, a mountain of Torridonian sandstone capped by Cambrian quartzite, rises from a rough platform of Lewisian Gneiss. The transgression of Cambrian over Torridonian strata can be traced along the flanks of the mountains till, in the left centre middle-distance, the Torridonian is completely cut out and the Cambrian rests directly on the gneiss. In the centre distance and on the left, Lewisian Gneiss carried on a major thrust-plane rests on Cambrian strata   ..   .. *Frontispiece*

PLATE   II. Geological map of the Northern Highlands   ..   .. *Facing page* 1

PLATE III. A. Dark banded gneiss cut by granitic gneiss. Cape Wrath, Sutherland (B4) 8

          B. Relict hills of Torridon Sandstone resting on Lewisian Gneiss. Looking south-east from Stoer, Lochinver, Sutherland (C3119) 8

PLATE IV. A. Mountain composed of flaggy siliceous granulite in lower part, muscovite-biotite-gneiss in higher part; Moine Series. Sgurr nan Clach Geala (3,637 ft), from the north; Fannich Forest, Ross-shire (B789)   9

          B. Folded Torridon Sandstone (dark) and Cambrian quartzite (light) in the post-Cambrian thrust-zone. On right of crest, Torridonian sandstone rests on Cambrian quartzite along a steep thrust-plane. Beinn Liath Mhòr, Achnashellach, Ross-shire (B138)   9

PLATE   V. Coast scenery of the Middle Old Red Sandstone, Caithness ..
          A. Stacks of Duncansby, composed of John o' Groats Sandstone (B865)   80

          B. Arch eroded in purple and red mudstones, red sandstone above. The Needle, from south side of Ashy Geo (B890)   .. 80

PLATE VI. A. Jurassic strata in beach, faulted down against Old Red Sandstone in cliff. Port an Righ, Cromarty (C1920) 81

          B. Lateral and terminal moraines. Lochan an Iasgaich, Ross-shire (B94) 81

PLATE VII. Fault-map of the Northern Highlands   92

PLATE VIII. A. Post-glacial gorge in Middle Old Red Sandstone conglomerate. R. Beauly at Kilmorack (C1284) 96

          B. Raised Beaches. 100-ft beach, and cliff and platform of 25-ft beach. Hilton of Cadboll, Ross-shire (C1924)   96

THE NORTHERN HIGHLANDS

I. INTRODUCTION

THE Northern Highlands of Scotland is the region which lies west of the Great Glen and its seaward continuations, the Moray Firth and the Firth of Lorne (Fig. 1). It includes the Inner and the Outer Hebrides, but the Orkneys and the Shetland Islands are excluded. A small part of the mainland and much of the Inner Hebrides are composed of Tertiary igneous rocks, and the reader is referred to the handbook on the Tertiary Volcanic Districts for full description of these areas.

Physical Features. Scotland beyond the Great Glen is composed mainly of Palaeozoic and Archaean rocks on which rest fragments of Mesozoic strata and of volcanic rocks extruded in early Tertiary times. At the close of this volcanic episode the region formed part of a great continental block which was reduced by denudation to a peneplane and later elevated into a high tableland with a watershed running in a north-north-easterly direction. Following on the uplift dissection by river action progressed vigorously. The Northern Highlands thus constitute part of a dissected plateau, the height of which averages now about 2,000 ft above sea level but varies from considerably over this level in southern Inverness-shire to about 1,500 ft in central Sutherlandshire (Fig. 1). The plateau before dissection appears to have had a more gradual and longer slope to the east than to the west. Large eastward-flowing consequent streams eroded valleys which have ever since guided the course of the main streams. The westward-flowing consequent rivers, not so long but more active, in course of time cut back through the watershed and captured the headwaters of the eastern drainage. In this way were developed the through valleys, which are now the regular, and only convenient, land routes from east to west.

Topographic description of the Northern Highlands falls naturally under three heads: (i) the area east of the watershed; (ii) the narrow strip running close to the watershed, from Loch Eireboll to Loch Alsh; (iii) the western seaboard and the Hebridean archipelago.

(i) The original easterly consequent drainage is exemplified by the Helmsdale valley, the Loch Shin hollow, the Strath Oykell and Strath Conon valleys, and the east-and-west valleys of southern Inverness-shire. Subsequent drainage towards the north-east and south-west was developed along the strike of the less resistant rocks and along north-easterly crush-lines. The most important valleys of this system lie along the lines of the Great Glen Fault and of the powerful parallel dislocation which skirts the eastern coast of Sutherland. Along these lines erosion was aided by the presence of sediments of Old Red Sandstone and Mesozoic age, and the broad shallow arms of the sea, or firths of Dornoch, Cromarty, and Moray represent submerged portions of these valleys. In the south, drainage along the Great Glen hollow captured the easterly-flowing rivers of Ardgour. Capture by subsequent streams is exemplified also in the interior by the Rivers Naver and Glas (Fig. 1).

Within the blocks cut out by the river-systems the smaller scale topography is fashioned under the influence of the geological structure. The county of Caithness is mainly a smooth low tableland built of flagstones of Old Red Sandstone age, but outliers of Old Red conglomerates and sandstones which rest on the Moine Schists west of Golspie and Brora, at Morven (Caithness), the Griams, and Meall a' Chrianain, form mountains more or less isolated during dissection of the high plateau. Within the outcrop of Moine Schists stretching from the Pentland Firth to Morvern (Argyll) a less rugged topography is produced by the siliceous granulite than by the mica-schist. Local geological structure is responsible for the mighty escarpments of Ben Hope (3,040 ft) and Ben Klibrick (3,164 ft) in North Sutherland, and the pinnacles

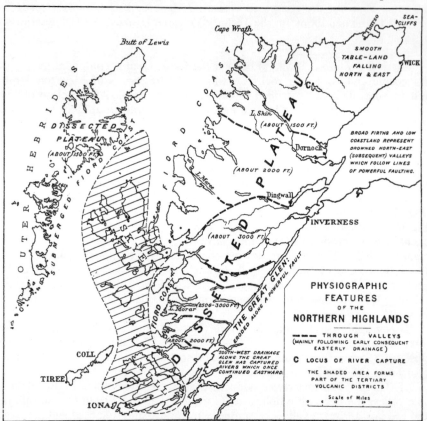

FIG. 1. *Boundaries and physiography of the Northern Highlands.*

of Ben Loyal rising from the monotonous moors south of Tongue reflect the intrusive character of the alkali-granite of which it is composed.

(ii) The strip of wild and desolate country running close to the west of the watershed from Loch Eireboll to Loch Alsh follows the outcrop of Cambrian sediments and of the great thrusts on which the Moine Schists were carried north-westwards over the Cambrian, Torridonian, and Lewisian formations. The distinctive topographic features of the belt are the westwardly facing escarpments above thrust-planes and the mountains, such as Ben More Assynt (3,273 ft) and Beinn Eighe (3,180 ft), formed by the protective agency of Cambrian quartzite.

(iii) The formation of the Hebridean archipelagoes involved three processes, erosion of westerly and north-westerly valleys on the north-west slope of the old tableland, followed by block-subsidence and relative rise of sea on land. The Outer Hebrides are built of a ridge of Lewisian Gneiss which is divided by a deep channel from the Inner Hebrides and the mainland. By submergence of the old valleys this ridge has been divided into numerous islands and only slight continuation of the process is required to subdivide still further the Lewis along the line of Lochs Resort and Erisort. The fiords of the Hebrides and western Scotland have been generally regarded as submerged valleys over-deepened by glacial action, but Professor Gregory has advanced the hypothesis that they originated along a network of gaping tension clefts. They are characteristically narrow and steep-walled, run generally north-west and south-east and have shorter east-west and north-south branches. They frequently possess a threshold near the entrance, and sink on the landward side to depths much greater than are found in the seaward continuations. The great inland lochs of the region repeat many of the characters of fiords. They have the same directions, straight course, steep banks, and great depth. Thus, Loch Morar, the deepest loch in Scotland, has a maximum depth of 1,015 ft, though its surface is only 30 ft above sea level. The largest loch in the region, Loch Shin, occupies a valley overdeepened by glacial action.

The distinctive local topographic features of the western area are best described under the next section.

Scenery.—Along the ridge of the Outer Hebrides rise rugged and jagged mountains of Lewisian Gneiss which in Harris attain a height of over 2,600 ft. The lower ground is intensely ice-worn and presents the rounded, bossy, tarn-dotted type of scenery which is characteristic also of the gneiss surface of western Sutherland. Along the north-west seaboard of the mainland the Torridon Sandstone builds mighty brown mountains which, in the north, rise high above the gneiss, and towards the south descend in precipitous cliffs to the sea. Eastward, Cambrian quartzite forms snowy caps on the mountains, and along the thrust-zone builds lofty, barren, scree-clad ridges among which green oases coincide with the outcrops of limestone. East of the watershed in central Sutherland ice-smoothed rounded mountains and ridges rise from a wilderness of peat. More interesting is the scenery of Ross and Inverness where a generally greater altitude and greater variety of rock-types yield a more rugged and grander type of mountain scenery. On the lower ground towards the east coast wide grassy and wooded straths lead to the sea through ice-smoothed and moraine-clad valleys or through picturesque post-Glacial ravines. Along the eastern seaboard the low-lying rich agricultural land round Dingwall and Tain narrows northward against the scarp formed by the powerful dislocation which reaches the sea at the red granite cliffs north of Helmsdale. Caithness, inland a dreary plain, is famous for its sheer sea-cliffs and sea-girt stacks.

Summary of the Geology. The various geological formations which appear in the Northern Highlands are shown in the table on page 5. Their areas of outcrop, the positions of the major unconformities, the facies of sedimentation and the episodes of hypabyssal and plutonic intrusion are also noted. With the exception of some hornblendic gneisses of doubtful origin in the Moine Series and a small number of vents cutting the Old Red Sandstone of Caithness, volcanic rocks are represented only in the Tertiary era (see British Regional

Geology: Scotland: Tertiary Volcanic Districts). The major structural features of the Northern Highlands are shown in horizontal section on Fig. 2 (p. 6). For a summary of research on the pre-Tertiary geology of the Northern Highlands between 1936 and 1957 a recent publication may be consulted (Phemister, 1958); this paper deals with the metamorphic rocks, the post-Cambrian Thrust Zone (erroneously referred to as the pre-Cambrian Thrust Zone, op. cit. p. 53 and p. 70), the Torridonian, Old Red Sandstone, and Mesozoic sediments, and the major faults.

REFERENCES

1774. PENNANT, T. *A Tour in Scotland and Voyage to the Hebrides*, vol. ii. Chester.
1819. MACCULLOCH, J. *A Description of the Western Islands of Scotland*, vols. ii, iii, and iv. Edinburgh.
1865. GEIKIE, Sir A. *The Scenery of Scotland*. London. (3rd Edition, 1901).
1886. CADELL, H. M. *The Geology and Scenery of Sutherland*. Edinburgh. (2nd Edition, 1896).
1902. MACKINDER, H. J. *Britain and the British Seas*. Oxford. (2nd Edition, 1907).
1907. HINXMAN, L. W. The Rivers of Scotland: The Beauly and Conon. *Scot. Geogr. Mag.*, vol. xxiii, p. 192.
1908. TARR, R. S. Glacial Erosion in the Scottish Highlands. *Scot. Geogr. Mag.*, vol. xxiv, p. 575.
1910. MURRAY, Sir J., and L. PULLAR. *Bathymetrical Survey of the Scottish Freshwater Lochs*, vols. i-vi. Edinburgh.
1910. PEACH, B. N., and J. HORNE. The Scottish Lakes in Relation to the Geological Features. In MURRAY, Sir J., and L. PULLAR. *Bathymetrical Survey of the Scottish Freshwater Lochs*, vol. i, p. 439.
1913. GREGORY, J. W. *The Nature and Origin of Fiords*. London.
1914. OGILVIE, A. G. Physical Geography of the Entrance to the Inverness Firth. *Scot. Geogr. Mag.*, vol. xxx, p. 21.
1916. BAILEY, E. B. In The Geology of Ben Nevis and Glencoe (Explanation of Sheet 53). *Mem. Geol. Surv.*, p. 4.
1923. OGILVIE, A. G. The Physiography of the Moray Firth Coast. *Trans. Roy. Soc. Edin.*, vol. liii, pt. ii, 1923, p. 377.
1923-1934. JEHU, T. J., and R. M. CRAIG. Geology of the Outer Hebrides. Parts I, II, III, IV and V, in *Trans. Roy. Soc. Edin.*, vol. liii, p. 419; vol. liii, p. 615; vol. liv, p. 467; vol. lv, p. 457, and vol. lvii, p. 839.
1926. SCOTT, J. F. General Geology and Physiography of Morvern. *Trans. Geol. Soc. Glasgow*, vol. xviii, pt. i, p. 149.
1927. GREGORY, J. W. The Fiords of the Hebrides. *Geogr. Journ. London*, vol. lxix, p. 193.
1928. OGILVIE, A. G. *Great Britain: Essays in Regional Geography*. Chap. XXI, The Highlands and Hebrides, by A. Stevens. Cambridge.
1930. PEACH, B. N., and J. HORNE. *Chapters on the Geology of Scotland*. Oxford.
1934. BAILEY, E. B. The Interpretation of Scottish Scenery. *Scot. Geogr. Mag.*, vol. l, p. 308.
1936. SÖLCH, J. Geomorphologische Probleme der schottischen Hochland. *Mitt. geogr. Ges. Wien*, Bd. 79, p. 32.
1949. LINTON, D. L. Watershed Breaching by Ice in Scotland. *Trans. Inst. Brit. Geogr.*, no. 15, p. 1.
1950. THOMPSON, H. R. Some Corries of North-West Sutherland. *Proc. Geol. Assoc.*, vol. lxi, p. 145.
1950. WOOLDRIDGE, S. W. The Upland Plains of Britain: their Origin and Geographical Significance. *Advanc. Sci.*, vol. vii, no. 26, p. 162.
1951. LINTON, D. L. Problems of Scottish Scenery. *Scot. Geogr. Mag.*, vol. lxvii, p. 65.
1951. ALLAN, D. A. The Scottish Scene. *Advanc. Sci.*, vol. viii, no. 31, p. 261.
1952. HOLTEDAHL, O. A Comparison of a Scottish and a Norwegian Shelf Area. *Trans. Edin. Geol. Soc.*, vol. xv, p. 214.
1952. STEERS, J. A. The Coastline of Scotland. *Geogr. Journ.*, vol. 118, p. 180.
1953. HOLTEDAHL, O. On the Oblique Uplift of some Northern Lands. *Norsk geogr. Tidsskr.*, Bd. xiv, p. 132.
1953. DURY, G. H. A Glacial Breach in the North Western Highlands. *Scot. Geogr. Mag.*, vol. lxix, p. 106.
1954. AUDEN, J. B. Drainage and Fracture Patterns in North-West Scotland. *Geol. Mag.*, vol. xci, p. 337.
1956. BOYD, A. J. The Evolution of the Drainage of the Fionn Loch Area, Sutherland. *Trans. Edin. Geol. Soc.*, vol. xvi, p. 229.
1958. PHEMISTER, J. Summary of Recent Research on the Pre-Tertiary Geology of the Northern Highlands. *Trans. Geol. Soc. Glasgow*, vol. xxiii, p. 53.

ERA	SYSTEM and SERIES		AREA (Sq. miles)	OBSERVED UNCONFORMITIES	CONDITIONS OF DEPOSITION	INTRUSIVE IGNEOUS ROCKS
QUATERNARY	RECENT AND PLEISTOCENE	{ ALLUVIUM, BLOWN SAND, Etc. / RAISED BEACH SAND AND GRAVEL / BOULDER CLAY, MORAINE }	Widely distributed	Unconformable on dissected plateau of Tertiary and earlier rocks	Fluviatile: sub-aerial / Marine / Fluvio-glacial / Glacial	
TERTIARY	EOCENE: (mainly IGNEOUS)		900	Unconformable on Upper Cretaceous, Trias, etc.	Sub-aerial: volcanic and lacustrine	*GRANOPHYRE AND GABBRO STOCKS; ACID AND BASIC RING-INTRUSIONS; BASIC DYKES*
MESOZOIC	CRETACEOUS:	UPPER	2(?)	{ Unconformable on Jurassic, Trias, and Moine Schists	Marine	
	JURASSIC	KIMMERIDGE CLAY / CORALLIAN / OXFORD CLAY / KELLAWAYS ROCK / ESTUARINE SERIES / INFERIOR OOLITE / LIAS	90	{ Unconformable on Trias, Cambrian, Torridonian, and Metamorphic Rocks. Several intra-formational unconformities	Marine / Estuarine	
	TRIAS	RHAETIC	10(?)	{ Unconformable on Carboniferous, Cambrian, Torridonian, and Metamorphic Rocks	Marine / Continental	*CAMPTONITE DYKES (? Age) / QUARTZ-DOLERITE DYKES AND BOSSES*
UPPER PALAEOZOIC	PERMIAN OR PERMO-CARBONIFEROUS (INTRUSIVE ROCKS only)		—	Relation to older rocks not seen	Lagoonal or Deltaic	
	CARBONIFEROUS		0·2		Lagoonal or Deltaic	
	OLD RED SANDSTONE	UPPER / MIDDLE	50 / 950	Unconformable on Middle Old Red / Unconformable on Moine Schists	Conti-nental { Sub-aerial Flood-plain / Lacustrine	
		LOWER (INTRUSIVE ROCKS only. Possibly in part of Caledonian age)	—		—	*'NEWER' GRANITE BATHOLITHS, STOCKS, DYKES, BOSSES, SHEETS. ALKALINE LACCOLITHS, SHEETS DYKES*

CALEDONIAN OROGENIC (MOUNTAIN-BUILDING) PERIOD

ERA	SYSTEM and SERIES	AREA (Sq. miles)	OBSERVED UNCONFORMITIES	CONDITIONS OF DEPOSITION	INTRUSIVE IGNEOUS ROCKS
LOWER PALAEOZOIC	CAMBRIAN & EARLY ORDOVICIAN	220	Unconformable on Torridonian	Marine	*'INJECTION-GRANITE' SHEETS, Etc. (? Age)*
ARCHAEOZOIC	TORRIDONIAN	650	Unconformable on Lewisian	Continental	
METAMORPHIC	MOINE SERIES (Age uncertain)	3,450	Unconformable on Lewisian		*SCHISTS, GRANULITES and GNEISS derived from SEDIMENTS; INJECTION GNEISSES. Pre-foliation IGNEOUS ROCKS are mainly basic SILLS, but include basic and ultrabasic BOSSES and acid and PLUTONIC MASSES*
ROCKS	LEWISIAN (Pre-Torridonian)	2,100			*ORTHOGNEISS derived from a GRANITE-GABBRO-PERIDOTITE COMPLEX forms the bulk of the Formation. SCHISTS, etc., recognized as altered SEDIMENTS cover 1 per cent of the total outcrop*

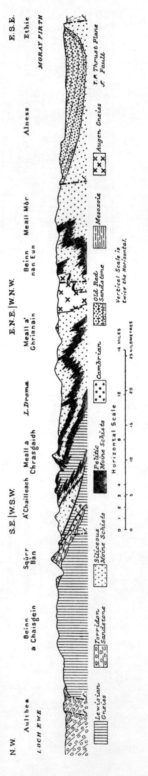

FIG. 2. Section across the northern mainland of Scotland.

II. METAMORPHIC ROCKS: LEWISIAN GNEISS

THE metamorphic rocks included in this formation build the islands of the Outer Hebrides, certain of the Inner Hebrides—Iona, Coll, Tiree and parts of other islands—and outcrop extensively in western Ross and Sutherland from Glenelg to Loch Eireboll (Fig. 4). The Lewisian Gneiss is of pre-Cambrian age and its antiquity among pre-Cambrian rocks is proved by the extensive denudation which it had undergone prior to the deposition of the Torridonian sediments (p. 38).

This complex of rocks includes paraschists and paragneisses which represent metamorphosed sediments, but the greater part is composed of orthogneiss produced by the metamorphism of plutonic igneous rocks which range from acid to ultrabasic in composition. It is usually difficult to establish the relative age of the sedimentary and igneous parts of the complex. In the islands of Coll and Tiree, however, evidence of intrusion of paragneiss by orthogneiss has been obtained, and accordingly in the following description the paragneisses are considered first.

Included also in the Lewisian Gneiss Formation are intrusions of granite and pegmatite, and of basic and ultrabasic rocks. While these are of later date than the earliest metamorphism of the gneiss, they are nevertheless of pre-Torridonian age, and often exhibit foliation.

PARAGNEISSES

Metamorphosed sedimentary rocks (Fig. 4) are found at Loch Maree, Gairloch and Glenelg on the mainland, in the islands of Tiree, Coll, and Iona of the Inner Hebrides, and at the south end of Harris and the north-east corner of Lewis in the Outer Hebrides. The original sediments consisted mainly of argillaceous and siliceous types in approximately equal proportions, and graphite persistently occurs in the more argillaceous members. Calcareous and dolomitic types are always important and richly ferruginous beds occur locally. The assemblage suggests a marine facies of sedimentation. In recent years paragneisses have been recognized in the Torridon district (Sutton & Watson 1951a, p. 245); they include quartzite and semipelitic and calcsilicate granulites and are older than the acid orthogneiss which has migmatitized them.

Loch Maree and Gairloch. The paragneisses of this district outcrop in belts which stretch in a N.W.-S.E. direction and measure up to eight miles in length near Gairloch, five miles at Loch Maree. An interpretation of their tectonic relations to the neighbouring rocks is shown in Fig. 3. Junctions with the orthogneiss are sometimes seen, but more frequently suspected, to be lines of pre-Torridonian thrust. Flinty crush-rock has been developed frequently in these zones of movement. The main rock-types are brown mica-schist and siliceous schist, with bands of graphite- and actinolite-schist and of quartz-magnetite-schist. Garnetiferous schists are fairly common among the mica-schists and an unusual type, cummingtonite-garnet-schist, occurs in the Gairloch area. Calcsilicate rocks interbanded with crystalline limestone and dolomite are common and may carry thin streaks of magnetite, pyrite or chalcopyrite, and rarely rutile. Near Carnmore, four miles N.N.E. of Letterewe, some bands of kyanite-gneiss and kyanite-biotite-schist occur within the orthogneiss. In both the Gairloch and the Loch Maree outcrops occur thick sheets of hornblende-schist and hornblende-chlorite-schist which are regarded as intrusive into the paragneisses rather than as contemporaneous lava-flows. They may possibly be of the same age as the basic dykes in the orthogneiss (p. 12). Sutton and Watson (1951a, p. 294) have suggested that Gunn may have been correct in inferring that the Loch Maree paragneisses were laid down on rocks subjected to an early phase of Lewisian metamorphism and were themselves affected by a later phase of pre-Torridonian metamorphism (*see also* Bailey, 1951b, p. 160).

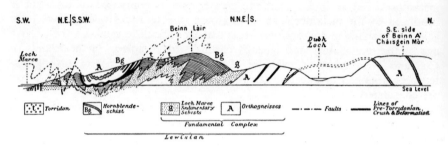

Fɪɢ. 3. *Section across the Loch Maree belt of paragneiss.*

Glenelg. The paragneisses of the Glenelg district include crystalline lime-stones carrying diopside, forsterite, and rare chondrodite, calcsilicate rocks, graphitic schists and gneisses, garnet-kyanite gneiss, and eulysitic rocks (*see also* pp. 12-13).

Inner Hebrides. In Coll, Tiree, and Iona metamorphosed sediments constitute a comparatively large proportion of the complex. Analyses of Coll paragneisses show that they correspond to arkose, dolomitic and impure sand-stones, and dolomitic limestone. Biotite-granulite and biotite-gneiss are the most widespread types and frequently contain garnet. Magnesian- and calc-silicate rocks are abundant and may contain hypersthene as an accessory mineral. In some bands this mineral becomes essential and eclogitic rocks of sedimentary origin are reported from Tiree. Similar material from Iona was regarded by H. H. Thomas as related to the orthogneiss. Graphite is widespread in the pelitic and calcsilicate gneisses and scapolite is a frequent constituent of the quartzo-calcareous members. Prehnite commonly replaces feldspar and biotite in the Coll gneisses. Among the purer limestones the Iona and Tiree marbles are well known as ornamental stones. The latter contain clots of the dark green pyroxene, coccolite, in a pink matrix of exceedingly fine grain which is due to intense crushing. In Coll quartzose gneisses are common and in Iona quartz-magnetite-schist carries small deposits of magnetite. It is worthy of remark that muscovite is a rare mineral in these altered sediments.

Outer Hebrides. In South Harris intensely folded belts of paragneiss with almost vertical foliation strike N.W.-S.E. Psammitic and pelitic members predominate, but lenticular beds of crystalline limestone are common, and with

A.—DARK BANDED GNEISS CUT BY GRANITIC GNEISS, CAPE WRATH, SUTHERLAND

B.—RELICT HILLS OF TORRIDON SANDSTONE RESTING ON LEWISIAN GNEISS. FROM STOER, LOCHINVER, SUTHERLAND

A.—MOUNTAIN COMPOSED OF SILICEOUS GRANULITE AND MUSCOVITE-
BIOTITE-GNEISS. SGURR NAN CLACH GEALA, ROSS-SHIRE

B.—FOLDED AND THRUST TORRIDON SANDSTONE (DARK) AND CAMBRIAN
QUARTZITE (LIGHT). BEINN LIATH MHÒR, ACHNASHELLACH

them are associated subordinate bands of calcsilicate paragneiss. The assemblage represents a series of sediments of rapidly alternating composition deposited in shallow water. Under high-grade regional metamorphism the non-calcareous members have been converted to quartzite, quartz-schist, and a variety of gneisses in which C. F. Davidson has demonstrated the common occurrence of garnet, kyanite, cordierite, and graphite. The calcareous members are represented by diopside-, forsterite-, and pargasite-marbles which are dolomitic and contain graphite and phlogopite. Kyanite-gneiss has been recorded also by Jehu and Craig in the continuation of the paragneiss belt which outcrops at the Toe Head peninsula. A phase of migmatization later than the regional metamorphism was responsible, according to Davidson, for widespread development of scapolite in the calcsilicate bands, and this author also holds the view that the lenticularity of the limestone bands is due to plastic flow under pressure at a period subsequent to the regional metamorphism.

Garnetiferous hornblendic and pyroxenic gneisses and pyroxene-rocks are interbanded with the paragneisses at the south-east corner of South Harris. It is suggested by Jehu and Craig that these rocks represent interbedded lavas or tuffs, but Davidson regards them as sills belonging to the adjoining anorthosite-metagabbro complex. Jehu and Craig describe from the north-east corner of Lewis strongly folded paraschists resembling the quartzose schists of South Harris.

ORTHOGNEISSES

Orthogneisses constitute the bulk of the Lewisian Gneiss in every area and the dominant constituent is a grey rudely foliated gneiss consisting essentially of quartz, feldspar, and one or more ferromagnesian minerals. The foliation may be only a vague orientation of the minerals, or a well-marked banding due to concentration of dark and light minerals (Plate IIIA). Within the pale bands quartz and feldspar are aggregated into lenticular folia. The gneiss is named after the predominant dark mineral. Thus pyroxene-gneiss is composed of quartz, feldspar (oligoclase or andesine), and a monoclinic pyroxene with subordinate hornblende and biotite. The feldspar of the hornblende-gneisses is usually a plagioclase similar to that of the pyroxene-gneiss. Potash-feldspar is not usually abundant except in the more acid biotite and muscovite-biotite-gneisses, and is then mainly microcline. The orthogneisses represent metamorphosed plutonic igneous rocks which vary in composition from granite to quartz-diorite.

The various types of acid orthogneiss have a regional distribution. Hornblende- and biotite-gneiss are predominant towards Cape Wrath, pyroxene-gneiss is typical of the district between Scourie and Loch Broom, while acid biotite- and muscovite-biotite-gneisses are commoner farther south, in Gruinard, Gairloch, and Raasay. The pyroxene-gneiss maintains its individuality over large areas, but the hornblende-gneiss and biotite-gneiss grade into one another and are usually not separable into large distinct areas. Hornblende-gneiss graduates into pyroxene-gneiss from which it is produced, in certain cases, by secondary replacement of pyroxene by hornblende.

The orthogneiss is rich in basic and ultrabasic components. The latter occur mostly as lenticles from one inch to several yards in thickness and as bands which can in some cases be traced for one-third of a mile. They are composed generally of biotite and hornblende, the former usually forming the skin of the

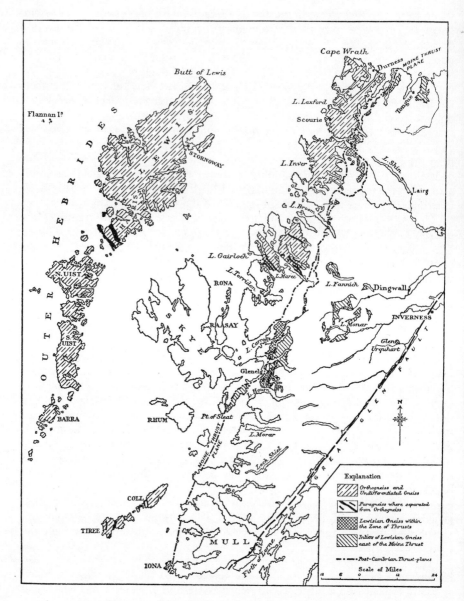

FIG. 4. *Distribution of the Lewisian Gneiss.*

lenticle. Other varieties are pyroxenites, which may contain hornblende and olivine or serpentine and occasionally carry needles of anthophyllite. They commonly show alternating concentration of the chief minerals in parallel bands. Near Scourie ultrabasic rocks are associated with basic types to form large masses of very variable composition, the ultrabasic members comprising pyroxenite, hornblendite, peridotite, and serpentine. Dunite and anthophyllite-carbonate-rock are also known. Garnet is often abundant in the ultrabasic masses; orthorhombic pyroxene is less common but locally abundant, while spinel is an almost invariable constituent of banded pyroxenites. Locally the ultrabasic masses are converted to talc, which may occur in workable quantity.

Like the ultrabasic, the basic members of the complex form small lenses, bands or lumps in the gneiss and also build large masses up to half a mile in length. In some areas these masses and lumps are sufficiently numerous to form half the bulk of the orthogneiss. The basic masses are often veined by the acid gneiss and at the edges the veins may become so numerous that the two types merge into one another. In every district it is found that the acid is later than the basic member, though chilling is never apparent. The banding, enclosure and veining of acid and basic members is not due to dynamic action but is an original structure arising from such processes as segregation of basic minerals and invasion of consolidated rock by acid magma, and probably is also a consequence of original heterogeneous distribution of liquid acid and basic material.

The basic members of the complex include pyroxene-feldspar and horn-blende-feldspar rocks, and, rarely, diorites. Usually they are massive and unfoliated or only rudely foliated. The pyroxene-feldspar rocks are most largely developed in association with the pyroxene-gneiss of the Scourie and Lochinver districts; they include pyroxene-granulites with variable content of garnet and hypersthene, hypersthene-augite rocks of Baltimore gabbro type, and augite-feldspar rocks with typical gabbroic texture. The hornblende-bearing types occur in association both with the pyroxene-gneisses and with the hornblende- and biotite-gneisses, and are, therefore, much more common than the pyroxenic types. They are classed as amphibolites and often carry garnet or epidote. Pale green pyroxene is a common accessory mineral. Foliated hornblende-feldspar rocks usually containing epidote, and sometimes garnet, are also common.

The orthogneisses of the Inner and Outer Hebrides are dominantly biotite- and hornblende-gneisses, with bands of more basic material, containing ande-sine feldspar and in places carrying small garnets. Basic orthogneisses adjoining and intrusive into the paragneiss of South Harris have been described in detail by C. F. Davidson. They consist of metagabbro (basic charnockite) inter-banded with and surrounding a core of anorthosite. The basic orthogneisses are in general garnetiferous. Lenses of massive eclogite usually sheathed in amphibolite are abundant in both metagabbro and anorthosite. Scapolitization of feldspar, amphibolization of pyroxene, and replacement of garnet by kelyphite are extensively observed and these changes are regarded by Davidson as connected with the later intrusion of the biotite- and hornblende-orthogneiss. Ultrabasic intrusions which are probably of the same age as the anorthosite-eclogite series form small masses in the paragneiss belt and are foliated and elongated in the direction of the foliation of the paragneiss. They are composed in varying proportion of olivine, hypersthene, diopsidic pyroxene, and edenite or hornblende with pleonaste and magnetite, and petrographically include peridotite, saxonite, and websterite. Intrusions of anorthosite occur also in many parts of Lewis.

Muscovite-biotite-gneiss and quartzo-feldspathic gneiss of more acid character than the usual orthogneiss occur in the islands of Iona, Barra, Lewis, and Raasay. In Lewis are found also flaggy muscovite-biotite-granulites which, though interbanded with granulitic hornblende-gneiss and clearly an integral part of the Lewisian complex, resemble the granulites of the Moine Series. For the distinction of these rocks from the Moine granulites Sir John Flett has suggested certain criteria (*see* Peach and Horne, 1930, p. 59).

LATER INTRUSIONS

Intrusive rocks which form part of the Lewisian Complex, but which are of later date than the foliation of the gneiss, are abundant (Fig. 5). They cut across the foliation and chill against gneiss. Long, broad dykes of basic and ultrabasic character are especially common in the Lochinver and Loch Broom district. The basic dykes strike N.W.-S.E. and are cut by the ultrabasic which trend W.N.W.-E.S.E. or W.-E. Petrographically the former include olivine-norite, hyperite, gabbro, dolerite, diabase, enstatite-diabase, epidiorite. The ultrabasic dykes are picrites, commonly serpentinized, and dunites occur in Harris. When altered by shearing movements both groups become schistose. The basic dykes pass into hornblende-schist, the ultrabasic into chlorite- and talc-schist. Similar dykes cut the gneiss in the islands of North and South Uist and in Harris. Unusual intrusive types are furnished by the microcline-biotite dykes of Assynt.

The most abundant intrusive rocks in the complex are granite and pegmatite. These are particularly common and large in the neighbourhood of Loch Laxford, and in Harris and Lewis. They cut both paragneiss and orthogneiss, and also the basic and ultrabasic dykes. They occur both as sills and as dykes, and in Lewis and Harris also form large plutonic masses. Foliated members may cut unfoliated ones, and it is concluded that foliation has been due to stresses acting intermittently during a prolonged intrusive episode. In their foliated facies they are described as granite-gneiss and are difficult to distinguish from the acid orthogneiss when the foliations of the two rocks are parallel. Sutton and Watson (1951a, p. 262) regard their intrusion and the migmatitization associated with them as a stage of the second metamorphism of the Gneiss (p. 13).

LEWISIAN INLIERS IN THE MOINE SCHISTS

In Ross-shire and Inverness-shire (Fig. 4) there occur east of the Moine Thrust-plane many outcrops of paragneiss and orthogneiss which have been interpreted as inliers of Lewisian Gneiss in the Moine Schists. These collectively cover an area of nearly 100 sq. miles. The orthogneisses comprise feldspathic, biotitic and hornblende gneisses, epidiorite and hornblende-schist, together with irregular masses of ultrabasic and basic material including eclogite, garnetiferous hornblende-gneiss, serpentine, and talcose schists. The para-gneisses include graphite-schist, limestone and calcsilicate rocks, kyanite-schist, brown mica-schist, scapolite-pyroxene-gneiss, biotite-schist, and biotite-granulite. Not every area contains paragneiss; for example, the inlier appearing in the Fannich fold shows only acid orthogneiss and epidorite. Occasionally a band of epidiorite or serpentine has been mapped cutting the foliation of the gneiss as the basic dykes do in the Lewisian Gneiss west of the Moine Thrust-plane, but since the inliers are involved in the isoclinal folding of the Moine Series, original structures are largely destroyed.

While the Lewisian inliers have been mapped out chiefly because of their lithological differences from the Moine Schists, evidence has been brought forward in support of the view that they underlie the schists unconformably. Somewhat rarely conglomeratic structure has been noted at the junction. This structure is well developed south-west of Glenelg and in Glen Strathfarrar (*see* p. 8). Other features suggestive of discordance have been observed; for example, various members of the Moine Schists come successively into contact with the gneiss; more frequently, one member of the schists transgresses several members of the gneiss. It has also been claimed that contact-alteration of the paragneiss of an inlier has been effected by the orthogneiss, while the adjoining Moine schists remain unaffected. Locally the original coarse foliation of the gneiss has been detected.

The largest and most accessible of the inliers occurs between Loch Hourn and Loch Carron, where the Lewisian rocks form broad belts separated by strips of Moine Schists. The foliation of both groups is parallel and the structure appears to be that of a great corrugated isoclinal fold with east-south-east dips. Typical Lewisian paragneisses are abundant and Tilley has recorded eulysitic rocks as associates of kyanite-gneiss and garnetiferous mica-schist, and regards them as altered siliceo-ferruginous sediments.

The Borgie inlier in the north of Sutherland contains no paragneisses but shows basic and ultrabasic dykes cutting the foliation of the orthogneisses. The latter are described by Teall as granular hornblende- and biotite-gneisses resembling the corresponding types west of the thrust-zone.

There has been much controversy in recent years on the age—Lewisian or Moinian—of the rocks mapped as inliers by the Geological Survey and on the nature of the junctions—conformable, unconformable or tectonic—with the surrounding Moine rocks; on p. 16 attention is drawn to some of the relevant publications.

FOLIATION OF THE LEWISIAN GNEISS: PRE-TORRIDONIAN
MOVEMENTS

Mainland. The dominant strike of the Lewisian gneiss (Fig. 5) is N.W.-S.E., but it can be shown in many areas that this is largely due to folding and movement of a comparatively late Archaean date, and does not necessarily indicate the original disposition of the gneiss. In the Torridon district and between Kylesku and Loch Broom the early foliation strikes N.N.E.-S.S.W. and N.E.-S.W. respectively and is folded gently and irregularly, while in the Loch Maree area it is flat or irregularly undulating. This early foliation was in existence before the intrusion of the basic and ultrabasic dykes.

Folding along N.W.-S.E. or N.N.W.-S.S.E. axes is best exemplified in the Loch Maree and Gairloch areas, where the zones of paragneiss and sheets of hornblende-schist are useful indicators. Crush-zones with the same direction are particularly widespread and powerful in this district and to the north and south of Lochinver. Within and adjacent to these zones the gneiss has been granulitized and the basic and ultrabasic dykes converted to hornblende-, chlorite-, and talc-schists. The new foliation induced in the gneiss is close and its direction is determined by the direction of the movements. Crush-lines directed E.-W. are also of importance. They are possibly younger than the north-westerly lines and like them have foliated and altered the dykes. Near Lochinver flat thrusts striking N.E.-S.W. are found.

Around Loch Laxford the N.W.-S.E. folding is steep and often isoclinal, and the dip is generally towards the south-west. Between Gruinard and Torridon the dip is generally north-east.

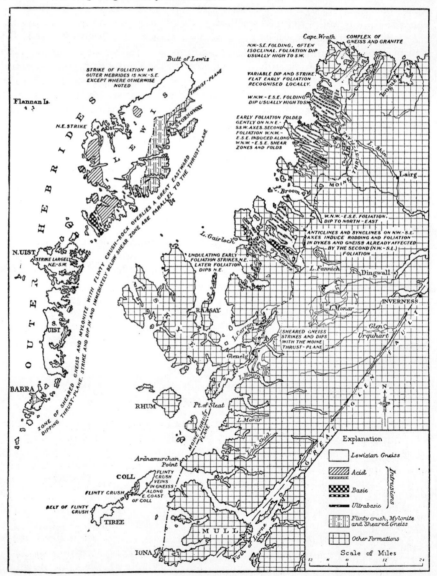

FIG. 5. *Foliation of the Lewisian Gneiss and distribution of pre-Torridonian ntrusions.*

Recent work in the Torridon and the Scourie-Laxford areas (Sutton and Watson 1951a) has dealt critically with the problems presented by the two styles of foliation of the Lewisian Gneiss. Sutton and Watson consider that the span of time between the intrusion of the basic dykes into a gneiss formation, which already had a long history, and the onset of the period of folding, recrystallization, and migmatitization which produced the banded hornblendic and granitic gneisses with N.W.-S.E. foliation was vast. They therefore distinguish two geological divisions of the Scottish Archaean. For the younger division they have proposed the generally acceptable term Laxfordian; for the earlier a suitable term is still to be agreed.

At many localities thin belts of flinty crush-rock and mylonites have been observed. Many are associated with the N.W. crushes, but some are directed E.N.E. It is not certain that their formation is contemporaneous with the N.W. folding and displacements, but their pre-Torridonian age has been ascertained.

Outer Hebrides. A N.W.-S.E. strike is very common, though in North Lewis the dominant strike is N.N.E. The most remarkable structural feature of the islands, however, is the zone of flinty-crush and mylonite overlying a thrust which skirts the eastern coasts (Fig. 5; Jehu & Craig 1923; Dougal 1928; Kursten 1957). This zone has a low dip to the east-south-east and in the gneiss immediately to the west a north-easterly strike has been induced. The age of the movements which mylonitized and sheared the gneiss is presumed to be pre-Torridonian (see p. 45). There is no evidence of the amount of the horizontal displacement. It is noteworthy that the thrust-zone is of the same type and has the same dip and strike as the post-Cambrian thrust-zone in the mainland.

West of the sheared belt the gneiss is traversed by N.W. lines of crush, which are possibly later than the flinty-crush belt. The rocks of Lewis almost everywhere show some degree of crushing.

Inner Hebrides. The strike of the Lewisian Gneiss is variable. In Coll and Tiree it is N.-S. and isoclinal folding is encountered. In Iona it is mainly N.E.-S.W. or N.N.E.-S.S.W. and is dependent on post-Torridonian movement. A north-westerly strike is, however, again found in the island of Soay. Coll, Tiree, and Iona are presumed to lie west of the Moine Thrust-plane but may fall within the post-Cambrian thrust-zone. Flinty-crush on a small scale is fairly abundant in the islands of Coll and Tiree and epidotic crush veins are numerous in Coll and Iona. In part of a broad vertical crush-belt in north-west Tiree epidote is extensively developed.

REFERENCES

1819. Macculloch, J. *A Description of the Western Islands of Scotland.* Edinburgh.
1859. Murchison, R. I. On the Succession of the Older Rocks of the Northernmost Counties of Scotland. *Quart. Journ. Geol. Soc.*, vol. xv, p. 359; and Supplementary Observations *Quart. Journ. Geol. Soc.*, vol. xvi, 1860, p. 216.
1885. Teall, J. J. H. The Metamorphosis of Dolerite into Hornblende-Schist. *Quart. Journ. Geol. Soc.*, vol. xli, p. 141.
1888. Geikie, A. Report on the Recent Work of the Geological Survey in the North-West Highlands of Scotland. *Quart. Journ. Geol. Soc.*, vol. xliv, p. 389.
1901. Horne, J. Recent Advances in Scottish Geology. *Rep. Brit. Assoc.*, p. 615.
1906. Flett, J. S. On the Petrographical Characters of the Inliers of Lewisian Gneiss among the Moine Gneisses of the North of Scotland. *Sum. Prog. Geol. Surv.* for 1905, p. 165.
1922. Jehu, T. J. The Archaean and Torridonian Formations and the Later Intrusive Rocks of Iona. *Trans. Roy. Soc. Edin.*, vol. liii, p. 165.

1923-34. JEHU, T. J., and R. M. CRAIG. Geology of the Outer Hebrides. *Trans. Roy. Soc. Edin.*, vol. liii, p. 419; vol. liii, p. 615; vol. liv, p. 467; vol. lv, p. 457; vol. lvii, p. 839.

1928. DOUGAL, J. WILSON. Observations on the Geology of Lewis. *Trans. Edin. Geol. Soc.*, vol. xii, pt. 1, p. 12.

1930. PEACH, B. N., and J. HORNE. *Chapters on the Geology of Scotland*. Oxford.

1931. MACGREGOR, A. G. Clouded Feldspars and Thermal Metamorphism. *Mineralogical Mag.*, vol. xxii, p. 528. (Scourie dykes).

1932. STEWART, M. Notes on the Geology of North Rona. *Geol. Mag.*, vol. lxix, p. 179.

1933. STEWART, M. Notes on the Geology of Sula Sgeir and the Flannan Islands. *Geol. Mag.*, vol. lxx, p. 110.

1934. STEAVENSON, A. G. Some Geological Notes on Three Districts of Northern Scotland. *Trans. Geol. Soc. Glasgow*, vol. xviii, pt. 1, p. 193.

1936. ALDERMAN, A. R. Eclogites from the neighbourhood of Glenelg, Inverness-shire. *Quart. Journ. Geol. Soc.*, vol. xcii, p. 488.

1936. TILLEY, C. E. Eulysites and related rock types from Loch Duich, Ross-shire. *Mineralogical Mag.*, vol. xxiv, p. 331.

1937. TILLEY, C. E. The Paragenesis of Kyanite-Amphibolites. *Mineralogical Mag.*, vol. xxiv, p. 555.

1943. DAVIDSON, C. F. The Archaean Rocks of the Rodil District, South Harris. *Trans. Roy. Soc. Edin.*, vol. lxi, p. 71.

1947. HALLIMOND, A. F. Pyroxenes, amphibole, and mica from the Tiree Marble. *Mineralogical Mag.*, vol. xxviii, p. 230.

1949. PHILLIPS, F. C. Lineation in Moinian and Lewisian Rocks of the Northern Highlands of Scotland. *Geol. Mag.*, vol. lxxxvi, p. 279.

1951a. BAILEY, E. B. *In* Discussion of Sutton and Watson 1951a. *Quart. Journ. Geol. Soc.*, vol. cvi for 1950, p. 303.

1951b. BAILEY, E. B. Scourie Dykes and Laxfordian Metamorphism. *Geol. Mag.*, vol. lxxxviii, p. 153 and p. 301.

1951a. HARRY, W. T. On a cupriferous Lewisian para-gneiss. *Mineralogical Mag.*, vol. xxx, p. 542.

1951b. HARRY, W. T. The Glen Dessarry Marble and its Associated Calc-silicate Rocks. *Geol. Mag.*, vol. lxxxviii, p. 393.

1951a. SUTTON, J., and J. WATSON. The pre-Torridonian metamorphic history of the Loch Torridon and Scourie areas in the North-West Highlands, and its bearing on the chronological classification of the Lewisian. *Quart. Journ. Geol. Soc.*, vol. cvi for 1950, p. 241.

1951b. SUTTON, J., and J. WATSON. Varying trends in the Metamorphism of Dolerites. *Geol, Mag.*, vol. lxxxviii, p. 25.

1952. HARRY, W. T. The migmatites and felspar-porphyroblast rock of Glen Dessarry, Inverness-shire. *Quart. Journ. Geol. Soc.*, vol. cvii, p. 137.

1952. MCINTYRE, D. B. The Tectonics of the Beinn Dronaig Area, Attadale. *Trans. Edin. Geol. Soc.*, vol. xv, p. 258.

1952. RUTLEDGE, H. The Structure of the Fannich Forest Area. *Trans. Edin. Geol. Soc.*, vol. xv, p. 317.

1953. SUTTON, J., and J. WATSON. The supposed Lewisian inlier of Scardroy, Central Ross-shire, and its relation with the surrounding Moine rocks. *Quart. Journ. Geol. Soc.* vol. cviii, p. 99.

1953. WATERSTON, C. D. An occurrence of harmotome in north-west Ross-shire. *Mineralogical Mag.*, vol. xxx, p. 136.

1954. SUTTON, J., and J. WATSON. On the Status of Certain Lewisian Inliers. *Trans. Geol. Soc Glasgow*, vol. xxi, pt. iii, p. 480.

1955. BAILEY, E. B. Moine Tectonics and Metamorphism in Skye. *Trans. Edin. Geol. Soc.*, vol. xvi, p. 93.

1955. KING, B. C. The Tectonic Pattern of the Lewisian around Clashnessie Bay, near Stoer, Sutherland. *Geol. Mag.*, vol. xcii, p. 69.

1956. FRANCIS, G. H. The Serpentinite Mass in Glen Urquhart, Inverness-shire, Scotland *Amer. Journ. Sci.*, vol. ccliv, p. 201.

1957. KÜRSTEN, M. The Metamorphic and Tectonic History of Parts of the Outer Hebrides. *Trans. Edin. Geol. Soc.*, vol. xvii, p. 1.

1957-58. MACGREGOR, A. G., and others. In *Sum. Prog. Geol. Surv.*, for 1956, p. 45; for 1957, p. 41.

1958. FRANCIS, G. H. Petrological Studies in Glen Urquhart, Inverness-shire. *Bull. Brit. Mus. (Nat. Hist.)*, Mineralogy, vol. i, p. 126.

1958. RAMSAY, J. G. Moine-Lewisian relations at Glenelg, Inverness-shire. *Quart. Journ. Geol. Soc.*, vol. cxiii for 1957, p. 487.

1959. SUTTON, J., and J. WATSON. Structures in the Caledonides between Loch Duich and Glenelg, North-West Highlands. *Quart. Journ. Geol. Soc.*, vol. cxiv for 1958, p. 231.

See also Geological Survey Memoirs (pp. 103,104) on North-West Highlands, Glenelg, Central Ross-shire, and Fannich Mountains.

III. METAMORPHIC ROCKS (continued)

THE MOINE SERIES

IN this section three large groups of rocks are described—namely, the series of metamorphosed sediments known as the Moine Schists, the igneous rocks which were intruded into the Moine sediments prior to their metamorphism, and the composite gneisses formed on a regional scale by injection of granitic magma into the schists. Together these rocks outcrop in the Northern Highlands over an area, about 3,500 sq miles in extent, which stretches from the Great Glen west to the sea and north-west to that long line of dislocation, the Moine Thrust, which runs from the Sound of Sleat in Skye to Whitten Head on the north coast of Scotland. West of this tectonic line rocks referred to the Moine Schists occur only in the peninsula of Sleat (*see* p. 26). Except in this district of Skye and in the island of Mull, the Moine Series has no place in the Inner or Outer Hebrides. In the south-west the Series is overlain unconformably by Mesozoic sediments and Tertiary volcanic rocks. On the north-east, between Loch Ness and the north coast, the Series passes unconformably below Middle Old Red Sandstone sediments.

THE MOINE SCHISTS

Lithology and Petrology. The Moine Schists consist predominantly of quartzo-feldspathic granulites and mica-schists, and include as subordinate members calcsilicate granulites and a very few crystalline limestones. In central and northern Sutherland belts of hornblendic gneisses form part of the Series. Over its whole outcrop the Series presents a banded aspect owing to the alternation of more quartzo-feldspathic with more micaceous layers. This small-scale banding reflects in miniature the composition of the Series by alternating psammitic, pelitic, and semipelitic groups. Semipelitic schists are those which are too micaceous to be called quartzo-feldspathic granulites and not sufficiently rich in mica nor sufficiently schistose to be called mica-schists. Similarly, a semipelitic group is one which on the whole is neither mica-schist nor granulite, but may contain many bands of both.

The *psammatic* types vary from quartzose schists, rarely quartzite, to massive and flaggy grey quartz-feldspar-granulites which carry biotite or muscovite, or both. Biotite is not common in the quartzose schists and quartzites. Quartz and feldspar do not segregate into folia as is common in gneisses, and the less micaceous varieties are therefore often massive. The more micaceous members usually exhibit good plane-parallel schistosity owing to the distribution of micas in parallel orientation. Garnet is a common though inconspicuous constituent, and zoisite or epidote, apatite, zircon, sphene, and iron-ores are frequent accessories. The feldspar is typically orthoclase, but microcline is predominant in some areas. Oligoclase or albite is commonly present and may be as abundant as orthoclase.

The texture of the granulites is granoblastic and the principal minerals are equigranular. In hand specimen the rocks have a sparkling crystalline appearance. Larger grains of quartz and feldspar representing the remains of pebbly fragments are common. These grains somewhat rarely become so large and numerous that the rock is obviously derived from an arkosic grit.

17

Layers of heavy minerals are fairly common among the granulites and in some areas form bands up to half an inch thick. The minerals include zircon, garnet, sphene, epidote, orthite, ilmenite, and magnetite. They may preserve the rounded form due to attrition even though the associated quartz and feldspar are thoroughly granulitic. Adjacent layers may show concentrations of a particular mineral. For example, in Moidart, where such bands are conspicuous, some layers are composed almost entirely of sphene and magnetite.

Conglomeratic (*psephitic*) schists occur locally at the base of the Series at its junction with the Lewisian Gneiss inliers. For example, south-south-west of Glenelg such a basal conglomerate is composed of pebbles of quartz, feldspar, and feldspathic and epidotic gneisses enclosed in a matrix of epidotic biotite-schist, which locally contains hornblende and garnet. This band has been traced for three miles and varies in thickness from 20 to 30 ft downwards. In Glen Strathfarrar conglomeratic schist occupying a similar stratigraphical position consists of fragments of quartzite and quartzo-feldspathic granulite embedded in a scanty matrix of biotite-schist which is locally epidotic. The granulites are distinguished from those of the Moine Series by abundance of andesine feldspar.

Several recent publications express opinions on the nature of the supposed basal Moine conglomerate (Bailey & Tilley 1952; Sutton & Watson 1953; Ramsay 1956; Clifford 1957; Sutton & Watson 1959).

Conglomerates, well developed in the upper siliceous group west of Càrn Chuinneag, contain pebbles of quartz, alkali-feldspar, quartz-felsite, quartzo-feldspathic granulite, and scarce haematite-mica-schist. The granulites resemble fine-grained psammitic Moine granulite. The pebbles are often deformed and in this area the schists seem subject to less recrystallization and to more mechanical deformation than is usual in the Series.

In the *pelitic schists* felts of muscovite and deep brown biotite form the bulk of the rock. Schistosity is very marked and may be of plain or wavy type. The schists are black or silvery according as biotite or muscovite predominates. They contain a variable proportion of quartz and feldspar and when the proportion is high these minerals are aggregated into lenticular folia. The feldspar is an acid plagioclase.

Garnets are common in the mica-schists. They vary in size from the microscopic to crystals one inch or more across, one quarter of an inch being a usual diameter. They may be idioblastic or xenoblastic and the larger crystals form 'eyes', usually with tails of quartz, round which the felts of mica sweep. Staurolite-mica-schist is found, though rather rarely, in pelitic belts and kyanite has been recorded still more seldom. The staurolite forms idioblastic prisms enclosing many quartz grains. Sillimanite-bearing pelitic schists occur on Beinn Gaive, Moidart, and in Glen Gour, but this mineral is uncommon in the Moine Schists except where they are involved in granitic injection-complexes.

Semipelitic schist. Every gradation exists between mica-schist and siliceous granulite. The intermediate members, the semipelitic schists, have generally a pronounced plane-parallel foliation and are dark or grey according to the greater or less content of biotite. In another common variety, 'pepper-and-salt' Moine schist, the micas are distributed in a uniform and poorly orientated manner, and the rock has a speckled appearance and tends to be massive.

Minor Members. Zoisite-granulites are the most important of the subordinate components of the Series. Usually they are interbanded as laminae or bands, a foot or less thick, in the semipelitic schists, and are white or dark grey compact rocks, speckled with red garnet and dark green hornblende. They are frequently banded as a result of parallel disposition of garnetiferous, hornblendic and biotitic layers; the other constituents are quartz and oligoclase, and all are granoblastic except hornblende, which tends to assume a poikiloblastic habit. Varieties containing zoisite in long blades without definite orientation occur.

Epidotic bands and epidosites, which may carry pyroxene or amphibole, occur among the pelitic schists, and thin bands of calcite-garnet-granulite are common among the quartz-feldspar-granulites.

Crystalline limestones occur at Shinness (Sutherland), and at Rebeg and Blairnahenachrie (Inverness-shire). They are associated with hornblende-schist and vary from pure white or pink, coarsely crystalline marbles to calc-silicate rock composed of pale green amphibole, diopside, zoisite, calcite, quartz, sphene, and feldspar (microcline and andesine). In Ardgour (Argyllshire) a group of limestones and pelitic gneisses, composed of sillimanite-biotite-gneiss and various pelitic hornfelses, occurs at the margin of the diorite-gneiss of Glen Scaddle and Coire nam Muc. The limestones vary from almost pure marbles and wollastonite- and scapolite-bearing types to calc-magnesian silicate hornfelses (see Contact-alteration, p. 28).

Hornblendic gneisses form long lenticular belts which strike with the foliation of the contiguous granulites in central and northern Sutherland. The rocks of these belts are dominantly hornblende-gneisses, and a granulitic variety possessing a remarkably persistent plane striping, due to alternation of hornblendic and feldspathic layers or laminae, is very common. Coarse granular gneisses varying from oligoclase-gneiss to hornblende-rich gneiss are abundant. The group includes bands of hornblende-schist and massive hornblende-rock, and pyroxene-gneiss is found locally among both the plane-striped and coarse granular gneisses. Biotite-gneiss and garnetiferous biotite-schist containing much apatite and some hornblende are members of the group. Orthite and epidote are common accessory minerals and the latter becomes essential in some quartz-epidote-granulite bands in the striped gneisses. Acid members have been interpreted as granulitized pegmatites and aplites and only in these is potash-feldspar an essential constituent. The group shows close petrographic correspondence with the orthogneisses of the Lewisian inliers in Ross-shire and Inverness-shire and has therefore been described as 'Rocks of Lewisian Type'. G. H. Francis (1958) has made the most recent assessment of these rocks.

No evidence of unconformity between these gneisses and the contiguous granulites has been observed. On the contrary marginal interbanding is common. Narrow belts of Moine granulites are found within broad outcrops of the hornblendic gneisses and bands and thin layers of the latter occur in the granulites. Minor basic and ultrabasic pre-foliation intrusions are numerous within the belts of hornblendic gneisses and occur also, though in restricted numbers, within the adjacent granulites. The gneisses and granulites have the same dip and strike and share a common folding. For these reasons the belts of hornblende-gneiss are regarded as part of the Moine Series.

Hornblendic rocks occur also in the Knoydart and Morar districts of Inverness-shire (Richey and Kennedy 1939). They are banded, striped and massive gneisses of ultrabasic, basic, and acid types and are garnetiferous in

places. Not uncommonly, epidotic bands are associated with them and acid
biotite-orthogneiss is locally abundant. These hornblendic rocks are interbanded with sedimentary granulites and schists which can be matched in the
Moine Series; they are, however, interpreted by Kennedy (1955) as thrust
masses of Lewisian age (*see also* Lambert 1958, 1959).

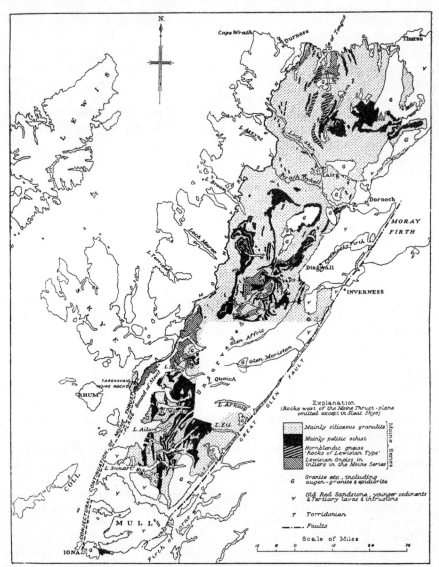

FIG. 6. *Distribution of the lithological groups of the Moine Schists.*

Origin. The Moine Schists represent a metamorphosed series of arenaceous
and argillaceous sediments containing subordinate calcareous and dolomitic
bands. This is borne out by chemical analysis and the following identifications
are made:

Siliceous granulite	= sandstone, more or less feldspathic.
Pelitic schist	= shale.
Staurolite-garnet-mica-schist	= shale of a more magnesian type.
Zoisite-hornblende-granulite	= siliceous marl.

Characteristic sedimentary features such as pebbles, layers of heavy minerals and current-bedding have been recognized, and passage of lines of heavy minerals across the foliation has been observed. Recent geological survey in Arisaig and Morar has demonstrated the existence in that region of unusually well-preserved original sedimentary structures, which include current-bedding, cross-bedding, ripple-marking, slump-folding, contemporaneous shrinkage cracking, contemporaneous erosion, and depositional lamination (Richey and Kennedy, 1939). It has been possible to deduce from the current-bedding that over a distance of 30 miles from Loch Sunart to Loch Nevis the prevalent set of the sediment-bearing currents lay slightly east of north. Slump-folding has been recorded also from Ardgour by Drever.

Direct evidence of the original nature of the schists has been obtained from the contact-aureole of the Càrn Chuinneag intrusion (p. 28).

Flett suggested that the sandstones were originally red in colour and that the ferruginous colouring matter was used during the metamorphism in the formation of biotite. The Series is perhaps of continental origin and has been compared with the Torridonian and Old Red Sandstone. It should be noted, however, that conglomerates are rare and that the granulites represent feldspathic sandstones rather than arkose. The Series appears to the writer to represent an estuarine or lagoonal rather than a flood-plain facies of sedimentation.

The group of hornblendic gneisses appears anomalous in this series of sediments. They may represent sediments of a ferruginous dolomitic type, they may be metamorphosed tuffs, lavas and associated minor intrusions, or they may be a series of sheets of banded igneous rock. No chemical analyses are available, but having regard to the field characters the writer prefers the second hypothesis. No trace of ashy or agglomeratic structure, however, is preserved. But the interbanding of hornblendic rock and siliceous granulite, the inclusion of markedly igneous types such as pure hornblende-rock and of definitely sedimentary types such as garnetiferous biotite-schist, the very narrow and persistent compositional banding, and the association with small basic and ultrabasic intrusions, seem most fully harmonized by a hypothesis of pyroclastic and effusive origin.

Thickness. Until recently only one estimate of the thickness of the Series had been made—namely, for the region of the Fannich Forest where the three lower groups are estimated as 4,000 ft, and the highest group as several thousand feet. The excellent preservation of original sedimentation structures in the schists of Arisaig and Morar has facilitated in that region estimates which are reliable but only for definite localities since the widths of outcrops may vary on account of sliding during the folding. The three groups of the Moine Series to the west of the core of the Morar anticline (*see below*) have the following magnitudes:

> Upper Psammitic Group, near Arisaig, about 12,000 ft.
> Striped and Pelitic Group, near Mallaig, about 3,500 ft.
> Lower Psammitic Group, near Mallaig, about 3,500 ft.

Stratigraphy and Structure. No general stratigraphical nor wide structural succession in the Moine Series has yet been established. Local structural sequences can be determined where distinctive pelitic, quartzitic or pebbly belts can be mapped. For example, in Northern Ross-shire the following succession exists:

> Mica-schist (contact-altered by the Càrn Chuinneag intrusion)
> Quartzose schists with bands of pebbly schist
> Garnetiferous muscovite-biotite-schist and gneiss
> Quartzose schists and granulites.

It is believed that the mica-schist first mentioned is the youngest member of this succession and that it occupies with the Càrn Chuinneag augen-gneiss the centre of a synclinal fold overturned to the north-west (Fig. 7a). The structure over a wider area is shown in Fig. 7b, where the Lewisian inliers offer a basis on which to develop the succession and structure in the schists. In this section it may be noted that the Moine groups are repeated in an orderly manner on the sides of the inliers; the rocks of the latter, however, do not show a corresponding symmetry of succession.

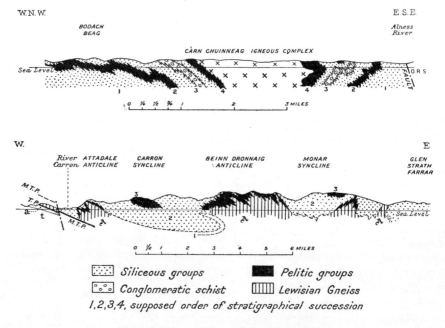

FIG. 7. *Sections in the Moine Schists.*

According to the Ross-shire successions postulated in 1912 and 1913 by the Geological Survey (Sheets 82 and 93), the siliceous granulites adjacent to the Moine Thrust-plane are comparatively high members of the Series. In northern Sutherland, however, there is an apparently steady upward structural succession eastwards from the outcrop of this dislocation, and it has been suggested that the Scaraben Quartzite, which outcrops on the border of Caithness and Sutherland, is the youngest member of the Series. Isoclinal folding on axial planes dipping E.S.E. is, however, so prevalent that even a regional succession of dips in this direction has no stratigraphical significance. The occurrence of the Lewisian gneisses of the Borgie inlier (p. 13) appears to offer a key to the solution of the structure in this district, but the asymmetric distribution of pelitic schists and hornblendic gneisses east and west of this inlier (Fig. 6) presents difficulties.

Successions recently proposed for central and south Ross-shire, on the basis of current-bedding and structural detail, do not confirm the Geological Survey successions of 1912-13; rocks which may be of Lewisian age are included either as stratigraphical units (Sutton and Watson 1954) or as tectonic lenses (Clifford 1957).

A local stratigraphical succession based on the evidence given by current-bedding was established in Arisaig and Morar (Richey and Kennedy 1939). The evidence demonstrates the existence of a great fold—the Morar Anticline—locally overturned on its west flank and with a general N.-S. axial trend from Loch Nevis to the Sound of Arisaig. The core of the fold is complex and has given rise to controversy. The sedimentary core-rocks, originally called 'Sub-Moines', were assigned to the Moines by MacGregor (1948); this view has now been accepted by Kennedy (1955) and Lambert (1958). No agreement has yet been reached on the stratigraphy and structure of the core, on the position and nature of the core/envelope boundary, or on the metamorphic state of the rocks inside and outside this boundary (Lambert 1959).

In Ardgour Drever has formed the conclusion that the limestones and pelitic hornfelses into which the diorite-gneiss of Glen Scaddle and Glen Gour is intrusive lie discordantly on the Moine Series and suggests their reference to the Dalradian Series.

The prevalence of isoclinal folding has been mentioned. The strike of these folds is fairly constant over large areas and the axial planes dip, in general, between east and south-east. Upon the large folds are superimposed subsidiary isoclines which are approximately parallel to the main structure, and in consequence the same band of schist may be repeated across the strike while a constant direction of dip is maintained. Pitch of the isoclines is frequent and causes interdigitating and lenticular outcrops. The isoclinal folds may be arranged in echelon with opposing pitch and the outcrops then show sharp bends or S-shapes and are liable to sudden change in width. Apparently simple anticlinal or synclinal structures are sometimes met, but the simplicity is illusory. Subsidiary folding of an unusual type is found near Altnaharra, Sutherland, where the schists are plicated by small flat isoclines whose axes lie in the direction of dip of the major structure.

The regional strike of the schists, as shown by the outcrops of the pelitic and siliceous groups (Fig. 6) on the Geological Survey maps, varies from N.-S. in northern Argyllshire to N.N.E.-S.S.W. in Ross and Sutherland. Important variations occur. (1) On the borders of Inverness-shire and Ross, that is, in the region of the Lewisian inliers, the normal N.N.E. strike gives place to broken sigmoids which may be explained by the superposition of a N.W.-S.E. system of anticlinal and synclinal folding on the normal system. (2) Adjacent to the Moine Thrust-plane the strike of the schists is controlled by the strike of the thrust-plane. Where the outcrop of the latter strikes E.-W., so also do the schists. (3) West and south-west of Lairg, Sutherland, an east-south-easterly strike is dominant. This great anomaly is associated with the eastward bulge in the outcrop of the Moine Thrust-plane in Assynt, with pronounced south-easterly deflections of strike in the schists approaching from the north, and with the sudden 'mushrooming', along a W.N.W.-E.S.E. zone on the south of this anomalous area, of a comparatively narrow pelitic belt which has coursed northward through Ross-shire with northerly strike. Steep thrusts striking W.N.W. are found in the siliceous schists to the east of this zone. Moreover, the schists in the anomalous area show conspicuous development of mullion-structure which pitches south-east. These phenomena suggest that during the thrust-movements the block of Moine Schists opposite Assynt was compressed from the N.N.E. and from the S.S.W. and its westerly motion retarded relatively to the schists on the north and south. Horizontal compression at right angles to the direction of thrust-movement is proved also by the well-known rodded schists of Ben Thutaig, immediately east of the outcrop of the Moine thrust-plane. The rods are due to the stretching of the cores of small isoclinal folds which are disposed parallel to the direction of thrust-movement. (4) A large fold striking E.-W. appears around Scaraben on the borders of Caithness and Sutherland.

In the 1948 edition of this handbook the view was expressed that the W.N.W.-E.S.E. system of folding is later than the regional N.N.E.-S.S.W. system, since the former is associated with the thrust-movements and these movements obliterate locally near the Moine Thrust-plane the effect of the N.N.E. folding. The latter is contemporaneous with the regional metamorphism of the Moine sediments into schists (p. 30). The W.N.W. system thus is associated with thrust-movements of Caledonian date, while the earlier folding has the strike proper to folding of Caledonian age. The two systems may therefore belong respectively to an early and a late stage of the Caledonian orogeny. It is possible, however, that the Caledonian orogeny merely emphasized and complicated earlier N.N.E.-S.S.W. tectonic lines. This must indeed be true if the regional stress metamorphism of the Moine Schists is pre-Torridonian. On the other hand, no pre-Torridonian folding with this strike, except very early undulations, is known in the Lewisian Gneiss west of the Moine Thrust.

A very different conception of the age and importance of the N.W.-S.E. system of folds is held by F. Coles Phillips (1937-1951). In a fabric study of the schists he has shown that the Moine Schists are B-tectonites, and he has correlated the lineation, rodding, and mullion-structure in them with the b-axes determined by fabric analysis. He points out that while the dip of foliation ranges from N.E. through S.E. to N.W., the pitch of the lineation and rodding is constantly into the south-east quadrant. These linear structures being parallel to the b-axes of the fabric and the latter being regarded as normal to the plane of the movement which has induced the orientation of the fabric, he deduces that the regional metamorphism of the schists was effected by compressive stress acting along approximately N.E.-S.W. lines. Therefore, since these directions of compression are prominent in the Lewisian Gneiss, the results of petrofabric study appear to him to support the view that the regional metamorphism of the schists is of pre-Torridonian age.

Phillips's inferences have been supported by G. Wilson (1953) but have been questioned and criticized by E. M. Anderson (1948, 1951, 1952) and by A. Kvale (1953) who believe that the direction of shearing movement, or transport, is parallel to the lineation and rodding. Other investigators disagree with some conclusions of Phillips and some of Anderson (e.g. Christie and others 1954; P. Clifford and others 1957). Views on the deductions to be drawn

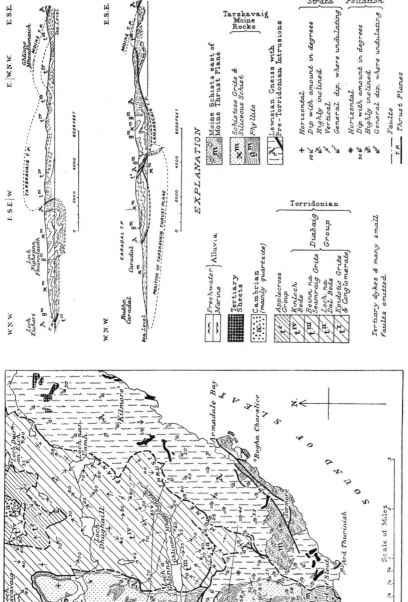

FIG. 8. *Geological map of southern Sleat, Skye; sections illustrating the occurrence of the Tarskavaig Moine Rocks.*
(In part simplified from manuscript map T. C. by Clough)

from details of structural petrology, including the time incidence of major and minor folding and cross-folding, are, in fact, still in a state of flux.

TARSKAVAIG MOINE ROCKS

It has been stated (p. 17) that rocks referred to the Moine Schists occur west of the Moine Thrust-plane only in Sleat, Skye. In this district phyllites and schistose grits carried on the Tarskavaig Thrust-plane were regarded by Clough as Moine rocks in a less highly metamorphosed condition than the schists east of the Moine Thrust-plane.

The rocks in question (Fig. 8) contain a basal group of alternating phyllites and sandy and gritty beds with calcareous seams containing clastic quartz and feldspar. The mica of the phyllites is in general finely divided muscovite, but in the outcrop east of the Point of Sleat round spots consisting of biotite and chlorite are common, while tiny garnets are numerous in the purer argillaceous seams. Overlying the phyllite group is a thick series of schistose grits with pebbles of quartz and of feldspar (mainly red microcline). The quartz pebbles are greatly elongated. False-bedding is readily observed in the grits. Epidote grains are abundant and may give the matrix a yellowish-green tint.

Clough held that the Tarskavaig grits and phyllites were in their metamorphic state before the thrust-movements took place and that these movements carried them westward a shorter distance than the schists east of the Moine Thrust-plane were transported. Tarskavaig phyllites now outcrop only a short distance from Moine schists (Fig. 8).

The Tarskavaig rocks were correlated with the Moine Schists by Clough because of the similarity in the stratigraphical sequence and in the character of their supposed basal beds and because of their similar relations to the Lewisian Gneiss. No representative of the epidotic grit and conglomerate which is constantly present at the base of the Diabaig group of the Torridonian in Skye occurs between the Tarskavaig rocks, or the Moine Schists, and the Lewisian Gneiss unless, as about one mile S.W. of Loch a' Ghlinne (Fig. 8), the junction is tectonic. On the other hand he pointed out the resemblance of the Tarskavaig rocks to the shales and grits of the Diabaig group and the similarity of their metamorphic grade to that of Torridonian sediments involved in the intense folding in advance of the Moine Thrust between Loch Carron and Loch Alsh. Considering the claim for equivalence of the Moine Schists with the Torridonian, Clough contrasted the constancy of lithological character of the schists with the variations of the Torridonian between Eriboll and Skye, and he remarked on the abundance of quartzite pebbles in the Torridonian as compared with the Moine rocks. Conceding that these differences may only be such as might exist between sediments contemporaneously deposited in different areas—the Moine rocks having been laid down far to the east of the Torridonian—he nevertheless was of the opinion that the evidence available to him did not warrant the conclusion that the Moine rocks represent Torridonian rocks. Research on the Tarskavaig Moines of Sleat, and the associated Moine and Lewisian rocks, has recently been critically reviewed by E. B. Bailey (1955).

PRE-FOLIATION INTRUSIONS

Ultrabasic. Ultrabasic rocks intrusive into normal Moine schists are described from central Sutherland. They form small bosses and, rarely, long sheets, composed of serpentine or of serpentine and epidiorite. Among the hornblendic gneisses of the same area similar intrusions are, however, numerous. They occur as bosses, more rarely as small sheets, and the commonest rock-type is a tremolite-chlorite-serpentine rock. Rocks composed dominantly of serpentine also occur, and varieties containing talc and anthophyllite have been noted. These intrusions are altered to talc-schist along shear-zones. Small masses and sheets of hornblendite, peridotite, and serpentine occur in the gabbro-diorite of Ardgour.

Basic. Minor basic intrusions, occurring as bosses and dykes and very commonly as sills, are widely distributed through the Moine Series. The sills may cut gently across the banding of the schists, but they share the folding and have been altered to hornblende-schist, hornblende-biotite-schist and chlorite-schist. The thicker sheets generally have massive centres of epidiorite or amphibolite. The basic dykes and bosses are of exactly similar type, but the bosses generally show less hornblende-schist and remain largely unfoliated. Originally of doleritic character the basic intrusions now rarely carry pyroxene, while basic plagioclase is limited to the less foliated portions. Epidote and zoisite appear abundantly in the hornblende-schists, and garnet, often in large crystals, is common but is erratically distributed in the amphibolites and hornblende-schists. Eclogitic amphibolite containing hypersthene has been described from the bosses intrusive in the hornblendic gneisses. As this fact has been used as an argument for the equivalence of these gneisses with the Lewisian it may be noted that the eclogites of the Lewisian occur as part of the plutonic complex and not in the hypabyssal intrusions.

Extensive bodies of basic igneous rock mapped as pre-foliation intrusions occur only within the Càrn Chuinneag augen-gneiss (p. 28), and in the Glen Scaddle—Glen Gour area west of Loch Linnhe. The Glen Scaddle and the Glen Gour (Coire nam Muc) masses have been described by H. I. Drever, who considers that they are parts of the same sheet or sill which have been separated by the effects of folding and denudation. This igneous rock, previously described as epidiorite, is termed by Drever a gabbro-dioritic rock with appinitic affinities. In general massive and retaining its original texture and mineral composition, it is intensely sheared in many places; foliation is then developed and pyroxene is uralitized. The intrusion is cut by dykes of amphibolite, pegmatite, and aplite, which are often sheared and foliated parallel to their length, and the surrounding diorite has the same direction of foliation. Small masses of appinite occurring in and graduating into the diorite have in places been impressed with a shear-foliation. Nevertheless, it is not certain that the intrusion of the diorite should be referred to a time before the regional metamorphism, since it contains zenoliths of amphibolite, quartzite, gneiss and, according to the Geological Survey, kyanite-gneiss also, and since limestones and pelitic hornfelses at the margin had suffered some degree of regional metamorphism prior to their contact-alteration. Moreover, it contact-alters a small mass of serpentine. The diorite is intruded at or near the junction of a limestone-pelite series which Drever believes to rest discordantly on the granulites. The latter are interleaved with and grade into sillimanite-gneiss which follows the margin of the igneous rock closely and encloses xenoliths of limestone and pelitic hornfels and which possibly owes its development to the effect of pegmatitic magma guided along the boundary of the intrusion. Drever's account of the Glen Scaddle area is reviewed by E. B. Bailey in a new edition of the Geological Survey Memoir on the Ben Nevis and Glencoe district (*in the press*).

Acid. Metamorphosed minor acid intrusions in the Moine Series are comparatively rare. Foliated sills of granite and pegmatite appear in certain areas, as, for example, west of the head of Loch Shin, Sutherland, and west and south-west of Inverness. The most important acid intrusions, exclusive of the injection-granites of Strath Halladale and Loch Coire, are the foliated igneous masses of Càrn Chuinneag and Inchbae, of which the former covers an area of 43 sq. miles, while the latter outcrops over fully 10 sq. miles. The large mass was regarded as a laccolith occupying the centre of a syncline (Fig. 7a), (p. 22), and it has been suggested that the smaller one of Inchbae was once connected with it before denudation had advanced to its present stage. According to R. I. Harker (1956) the Càrn Chuinneag augen-gneiss more probably represents an intrusive sheet intercalated in Moine sediments. The dominant rock of these masses is a coarse biotite-granite or granite-gneiss which is well known as the Inchbae augen-gneiss. The 'augen' or 'eyes' are large porphyritic crystals of orthoclase or microcline which are often an inch across and which on account of the pressure to which the rock has been subjected are usually disposed so that their long axes are parallel. Cataclastic effects are generally present and bands of fiaser material are common. The direction of foliation shown by the augen and the rudely lenticular arrangements of the other constituents are usually parallel to the N.N.E. foliation in the schists. The Inchbae mass is almost entirely built of this augen-gneiss, but the Càrn Chuinneag mass is composed of a number of different types (Fig. 9). Basic masses, consisting of metamorphosed but often unfoliated gabbro, diorite, and quartz-diorite, form the earliest component. Augen-gneiss and biotite-granite-gneiss, which grade into one another, form the bulk of the complex. Riebeckite-aegirine-gneiss, which occurs as a broad band or dyke crossing the summit of Càrn Chuinneag, is probably a late component. Garnetiferous albite-gneiss is a minor member occurring as narrow bands on the north-west shoulder of Càrn Chuinneag. It contains streaks of magnetite and cassiterite and may represent a metamorphosed basic segregation (*see also* Harker 1954b).

Contact-alteration. The Càrn Chuinneag augen-gneiss is in contact with Moine sediments of a laminated siliceous and argillaceous type along most of its boundary and has produced a contact-aureole which is in places nearly a mile broad. The tough hornfelsed sediments have largely remained unaffected by the regional stress metamorphism and show the original sedimentary lamination and current-bedding in a conspicuous manner. Markings interpreted as rain-pittings, sun-cracks, and ripple-marks have been observed. The characteristic contact-mineral is biotite, but in the more argillaceous layers small garnets are numerous and kyanite forms swarms of small needles in the more intensely altered seams. Chiastolite, often replaced by fibrous kyanite, and cordierite, replaced by muscovite, chlorite and kyanite, are of restricted occurrence. Gentle anticlinal and synclinal folds on north-westerly axes are preserved in the eastern section of the aureole. Beds conforming to these folds swerve sharply at the limit of contact-effect into the normal N.N.E. direction of strike of the schists and are concurrently converted into mica-schist. Both along the outer margin of the aureole and at internal positions where shearing has occurred, especially near the granite contact, conversion of hornfels to mica-schist can be observed. This process has been studied microscopically. In the beginning white mica is developed from potash-feldspar as minute flakes with pronounced parallel orientation. Later, the white mica becomes larger; biotite changes from red-brown to yellow-brown and is orientated; garnets become larger but fewer; albite appears and may become porphyroblastic. The aluminous minerals, kyanite and andalusite, are converted at an early stage into micaceous aggregates. With increasing stress these are

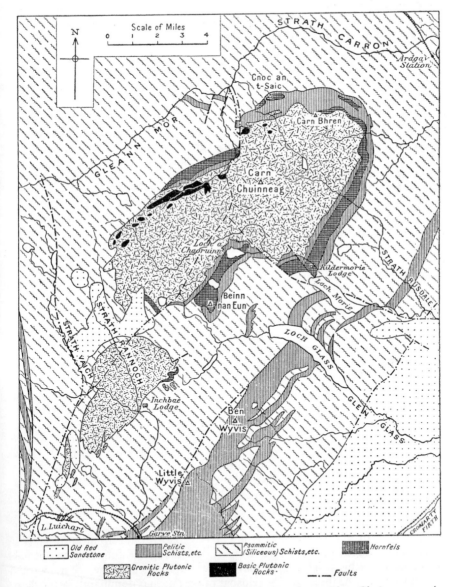

FIG. 9. *Pre-foliation intrusions and contact-aureole at Càrn Chuinneag and Inchbae.*

deformed to streaks and lenses which eventually merge into the micaceous laminae. Sedimentary banding is destroyed by development of films of mica across the bedding (*see also* Tilley 1935; Harker 1954a).

From the facts available the important conclusion is drawn that the metamorphism of the Moine sediments into schists was contemporaneous and essentially connected with the isoclinal folding on N.N.E.-S.S.W. axes.

Contact-alteration by the Glen Scaddle and Glen Gour gabbro-diorite (p. 27) has affected both limestone and pelitic rocks. In the altered limestones scapolite, wollastonite, garnet, pyroxene, and prehnite are of frequent occurrence. The pelitic hornfelses are banded and contain associations of cordierite with garnet, hypersthene, spinel, sillimanite, oligoclase, and corundum.

GRANITE-SCHIST INJECTION-COMPLEXES

Gneisses produced by the injection of granitic and pegmatitic material into the Moine Schists were first mapped as such by the Geological Survey in Strath Halladale on the border of Caithness and Sutherland. Later survey showed that the injection-gneisses or migmatites of this northern region have outcrops exceeding 700 sq miles in area. Similar gneisses have been recognized but not delimited in Central Ross-shire, and their outcrop may be continuous with the great injection-complex which extends through Inverness-shire and Northwest Argyllshire to the Sound of Mull. Recent mapping has shown that the injection-gneisses of this region occupy a north-south belt fully 50 miles long and at least 15 miles wide; the eastern boundary has not yet been completely surveyed. Pegmatitized schists have also been recognized in the Ross of Mull.

The gneisses composing the injection-complexes present great lithological variety in consequence of the varied ways in which the granitic material may invade the schists and also because of the diversity of composition of the schists and associated pre-foliation intrusions. The composite gneisses are coarser in grain than the ordinary schists and granulites and are in the main rocks to which such descriptive terms as banded quartzo-feldspathic gneiss, biotite-gneiss, augen-gneiss, and granitic gneiss may be applied.

Sutherland and Caithness. The injection-complex, centred on *Loch Coire* (Fig. 16, p. 62), stretches north and south for at least 25 miles and reaches 18 miles in width. It is separable into three parts: (i) an outer *Zone of Veins*, in which acid igneous rock occurs abundantly as sills; (ii) a *Zone of Injection*, in which the schists are intermixed with a comparable volume of granitic material; (iii) *Granite of the complex*, occurring in small outcrops widely scattered through the zone of injection. In the zone of veins the schists show enlargement of grain, intricate suturing of quartz and feldspar grains, increase in proportion of oliogoclase, and reddening of biotite. Within the zone of injection composite gneisses (migmatites) of three kinds are distinguished: (*a*) injection-gneiss, in which the igneous and schist components remain discrete though finely interbanded; (*b*) permeation-gneiss, in which discrimination of the igneous and schist components is not possible; (*c*) augen-injection-gneiss, which shows augen of feldspar and quartz set along the foliation of normal and permeated schists. The augen may be few and isolated, or may be numerous and joined by aplitic threads. The feldspar of the augen is dominantly orthoclase in the semipelitic, dominantly oligoclase in the pelitic gneisses. Sillimanite is common in the injection- and permeation-gneisses formed from pelitic schists.

Among the minor members of the Moine Series injection-metamorphism produces distinctive and marked change. Coarse glassy quartzites resembling vein-quartz arise from recrystallization of the more siliceous granulites. Calc-silicate bands acquire a vitreous lustre and show development of a basic plagioclase. Epidiorites and hornblende-schists do not readily form injection-gneisses but are susceptible to veining and transgressive penetration by the granitic material. When this process leads to complete incorporation of the hornblendic rock, poorly foliated hornblendic granite-gneisses are the ultimate products. When the individuality of the hornblendic rock is retained, the main effects are production of basic plagioclase and of a biotite-prehnite intergrowth. The mineralogical and chemical changes occurring during migmatization have been closely studied by Yu-Chi Cheng (1944).

The injection-complex of *Strath Halladale* (Fig. 16, p. 62) covers an area of fully 200 sq miles. The granitic intrusions form sheets which are more clearly separated from the schists, while permeation is less extensive than in the Loch Coire complex. As in the latter, a high degree of interpenetration of granite and schist and increase in quantity of granite are concurrent with increase in coarseness of the texture of the schists and with perfection of crystallization of sillimanite. At many localities in this complex siliceous granulites containing quartz-sillimanite knots (faserkiesel) are found.

Ross-shire, Inverness-shire and North-west Argyllshire. Recent survey in the western Highlands has proved that the injection-gneisses of the Loch Duich-Loch Hourn area are continuous with the belt of pegmatitic injection which runs north and south across Loch Shiel. The injection-complex of the western Highlands thus extends for a distance of 60 miles from the Sound of Mull north to Loch Duich, its width varying from about 10 to 16 miles. It appears to continue northwards, across ground which has still to be mapped, and in prospecting surveys for mica carried out during the 1939-45 war much of the pelitic gneiss of Ross-shire, for example in the Ben Wyvis massif, was classed as injection-gneiss.

In Ross-shire the lower pelitic group of the Moine Schists is a coarse muscovite-biotite-gneiss carrying quartzo-feldspathic augen and folia which were regarded by some of the original surveyors as segregations, by others as introduced pegmatitic material. The descriptions given in the memoirs explanatory of 1-inch Sheets 82, 83, 92 and 93 indicate that pegmatitization mainly affects the lower pelitic group of the schists and also that permeation-gneisses, if present, are rare. It seems that in this region the invasion of the schists by acid liquors is both less voluminous and intense and more selective than in the Loch Shiel and Loch Coire areas, and an endeavour has been made to interpret diagrammatically in Figs. 16 and 17 the evidence scattered through the memoirs. It should be stated, however, that some of the writer's colleagues consider that the area of injection extends much more continuously and extensively over Ross-shire than is shown on these figures. The selective association of pegmatitization with one particular group of schists, which is believed to be a stratigraphical group, throughout its widely separated outcrops, suggests that the injection-process accompanied or, at least, was not later than the folding.

The following types of injection-gneiss were described in 1910 by Clough from the Loch Duich-Loch Hourn area:—coarse psammitic gneiss mixed with pegmatite veins and lenses and containing augen of feldspar, pelitic gneisses intimately threaded and augened by pegmatite, and granite-gneiss. He appears to have been able to distinguish the injection-phase within the gneisses of the Lewisian inlier as well as in the Moine Schists. The Ràtagain Granite is situated within the injection-complex but is later than the pegmatitization.

The injection-complex of Knoydart, Morar, Moidart and Sunart has not yet been described in detail. The injection is of both lit-par-lit and permeation types, yielding banded injection-gneiss, augen-gneiss, and permeation-gneiss indistinguishable from those of the Loch Coire Complex. The parent body of the injecting magma is not exposed, but pegmatite and granite occur locally in cross-cutting veins and concordant sheets and lenses among the injection-gneisses, and are particularly concentrated along the 'great pegmatite belt', about $1\frac{1}{2}$ miles wide, which runs north and south across the north end of Loch Shiel. Between the Strontian Granite and Loch Linnhe, belts of coarse glassy quartzite occur and seem to have experienced the same type of recrystallization as similar rocks within the Sutherland complexes. Mineral parageneses associated with the injection-process include extensive development of muscovite both as porphyroblasts and augen, production of a transparent violet garnet to replace the deep red opaque garnet usual in the Moine Schists, and local development of sillimanite. Tourmaline and beryl may occur in the pegmatites. The Strontian Granite is situated within the injection-complex, and, though the intensity of injection in its vicinity is high, MacGregor and Kennedy have shown that the granite is of later date than the injection episode.

For more recent work on injection-gneisses, augen-gneiss, and granite-gneiss, papers by Y. C. Cheng (1944), G. P. Leedal (1952), W. T. Harry (1952, 1954), and the Summaries of Progress of the Geological Survey for the years 1951-1955 may be consulted.

Ross of Mull. Pegmatites and pegmatitized pelitic gneisses carrying tourmaline are abundant among the Moine Schists of the Ross of Mull (Fig. 17, p. 63). Bosworth considered the pegmatitization of much earlier date than the intrusion of the Ross of Mull Granite and regarded it as due to segregation of the quartzo-feldspathic constituents of the schists. It is possible, however, that the pegmatitized area represents an extension of the Loch Sunart injection-complex and it is noteworthy that, as in the latter, pelitic schists are very rich in muscovite.

Recognition of injection-gneisses in the Moine Series brings to the front the problem of the importance of such gneisses in the Lewisian. Isolated bands of schist and gneiss, especially kyanite-gneiss, and of limestone have been detected within orthogneiss. It seems probable that a proportion of the orthogneiss larger than is at present recognized may be of sedimentary origin. Clough, referring to the banded gneiss of the Lewisian inlier in the Glenelg district, states: 'the hypothesis which most commends itself to the writer is that the series represents a complex in which the oldest rocks are of sedimentary origin and have been injected and greatly altered by a variety of igneous rocks, intruded under peculiar conditions and considerable pressure' (Explanation to Sheet 71, p. 19).

Granites of the Injection-complexes, etc. The Strath Halladale Granite is composed of a concordantly intrusive assemblage of foliated and unfoliated sheets. The foliation was regarded by Horne and Greenly as the effect of fluxion as well as of earth-movement. The granite is in parts porphyritic and the phenocrysts of feldspar (perthitic orthoclase) may be arranged in parallel alignment. It contains a variable, often high, proportion of oligo-clase, and myrmekite is common. The thin sheets intrusive into sillimanite-gneisses may themselves contain sillimanite, which occurs as clusters of needles and as fibres enclosed in muscovite and quartz. Veins and dykes of aplite represent the last stage of the Strath Halladale injection-process. They are composed of quartz, orthoclase, and microcline and carry much muscovite and sometimes a few pink garnets.

Within the Loch Coire injection-complex bodies of homogeneous igneous rock are of small size and consist of medium- to coarse-grained biotite-granite in which oligoclase may be dominant over orthoclase. The largest mass within the outcrop of the complex is the Strath Naver Granite, a streaky biotite-granite which is locally contorted and sheared and encloses masses of sheared hornblendic rock. This granite cuts the injection-gneisses and therefore cannot be regarded as the source of their granitic component.

All the injection-complexes contain pegmatites, some of which are con-cordantly, some transgressively intrusive in the gneisses. They may carry muscovite or biotite and may contain oligoclase as well as orthoclase. Some are garnetiferous. Rarely they show foliation. Near Garve (Ross-shire) and at Loch Nevis (Inverness-shire) pegmatites have been worked for the large crystals of muscovite which they contain. At the Loch Nevis Prospect beryl is abundant, crystals up to 12 in. in length having been obtained. At Garve black tourmaline is common.

Augen-granite. Several sills of augen-granite appear within the zone of veins at Vagastie on the west margin of the Loch Coire complex. The sills are foliated but contact-alter the granulites. They are therefore included here among the injection-granites rather than among the pre-foliation intrusions, though their age relative to the regional injection is not known.

Quartz-veins are numerous outside the zone of veins of the Loch Coire and to the west of the Loch Sunart complex. They appear as ribs following the foliation of the granulites and sometimes are seen to shoot out from a cross-cutting trunk-vein. They may possess a granular appearance suggestive rather of quartzite than vein-quartz.

General Remarks. The outstanding structural feature of the injection-complexes is the concordance of injected material with the foliation of the schists. The magma was intruded at a time when the schists over large areas were under stress and in such a physical condition that they yielded along no especial lines of weakness but were equally penetrable along any of the planes of foliation. The abundant development of permeation-gneisses and the crystal-line continuity of discrete injections with the contiguous schists suggest that the schists were at a high temperature when intrusion occurred. It is possible also that folding movements under crustal stress were still in progress since the igneous material follows the lines of crumpling in pelitic gneisses and the more regular folds in the quartzo-feldspathic gneisses. Perhaps, however, the pressure of the magma invading the schists also played a part in the production of these folds. Clough noted granulitization and rude foliation parallel to the axial planes in a few of the igneous ribs.

The injection-complexes also contain many transgressive intrusions. From Horne and Greenly's admirable account it is clear that these were partly synchronous with, partly later than, the concordant injections. A vein, dyke-like on one side, may merge insensibly into the injection-gneiss on the other side. The later dykes or veins frequently show fluxion-structure parallel to the walls and transgressive to the foliation of the schists, but may in rare cases show the same direction of foliation as the schists. Fluxional or foliated veins may truncate the direction-structure of similar earlier veins. The later dykes may be emplaced along small faults which cross the injection-gneiss, but nevertheless show crystalline continuity with the wall rock along the fault. Therefore, though the country-rock was then sufficiently rigid to be fractured, it was probably still at a fairly high temperature. The complexes also contain cross-cutting dykes of granite, pegmatite, and aplite which show no directed structure whatever and possess clean-cut contacts with the country-rock.

Age of Regional Granitic Injections. The assumption is made that the injections in the various areas are coeval, and it is possible that the injecting magmas correspond to the 'Older Granites' of the Grampian Highlands. From the details given above, it is clear that at the beginning of the magmatic influx the schists were at a high temperature and were under considerable compressive stress transverse to their strike. Horne and Greenly, and later Read, therefore correlated the period of injection with the period of dynamo-thermal metamorphism of the schists. It is, however, a demonstrable fact that when the schists were invaded by the magma they were already in the same metamorphic condition as they are to-day outside of the injection-complexes. Horne and Greenly admitted the probability of this circumstance in the case of the injection-complex on the north coast of Sutherland, while in the Glenelg district Clough reached the conclusion that the pegmatitization was to a small extent concurrent with, but mainly later than, the folding. It is reasonable to believe that the period of granitic injection was synchronous with the period of dissipation of stress in the schists following on their dynamothermal meta-morphism, unless at some later period similar conditions of compressive stress and high temperature prevailed.

A pre-Torridonian age for the regional granitic injections is advocated by Read. The writer, however, considers that reasonable grounds exist for believing them to be of early Caledonian age. At that geological period the requisite condition of compression transverse to the strike is proved by the thrust-movements. Moreover, while appinites and foliated lamprophyres, the earliest of the 'Newer Granite' intrusions in Moidart and Morvern (p. 61), cut the injection-gneisses, the corresponding minor intrusions in Sutherland are regarded by Read as facies of injection-rocks, and unfoliated ultrabasic sheets probably of Newer Granite age are cut by aplites, granites and peg-matites which are presumably the latest phase of the Strath Halladale Granite. Recently Cheng has described from north Sutherland two groups of hornblendic intrusions containing appinitic members or facies, one group being of pre-injection age, the other contemporaneous with the injection granites. The foliation of some early members of the Newer Granite intrusions shows that the region had not been completely relieved of stress by that time (pp. 64 & 69). The existence of injection-complexes at the margins of certain of the Newer Granites, though small compared with the regional injection-complexes, indicates that a state of permeability still existed locally in the schists. It is, therefore, possible that the regional granitic injections represent the earliest manifestations of Caledonian igneous activity, and, occurring in the main contemporaneously with the thrust-movements, locally persisted into the beginning of the period of post-movement—that is, Newer Granite—intrusion.

AGE OF THE MOINE SERIES

The Moine Schists are intruded by igneous rocks of Lower Old Red Sand-stone, or possibly late Silurian, age. The time-interval between this period of intrusion and the period of deposition of the Moine sediments is uncertain, but during it the following events occurred: (i) intrusion of pre-foliation acid and basic igneous rocks; (ii) gentle folding, possibly only local, on E.-W. axes; (iii) isoclinal folding on N.N.E.-S.S.W. axes and accompanying dynamothermal metamorphism of the sediments into schists; (iv) formation of regional granite-schist injection-complexes within which the grade of metamorphism of the schists was raised; (v) development of the post-Cambrian thrusts and accom-panying retrograde metamorphism of the schists close to the Moine Thrust-plane. The dates of events (iv) and (v) are discussed elsewhere (p. 34 and p. 56). The relative age of events (i) and (ii) is uncertain; both were prior to the dynamo-thermal metamorphism. In the following pages the various hypotheses relative to the age of the Moine sediments and of their dynamothermal metamorphism are presented.

Age of the Moine Sediments. A summary of the facts and inferences, which have a bearing on this question, is presented below and should be examined with reference to the four hypotheses which have been put forward—namely, that the age of the Moine sediments is (i) Lewisian; (ii) post-Lewisian but pre-Torridonian; (iii) Torridonian; (iv) post-Cambrian.

(*a*) The Moine sediments belong to a shallow-water facies.

(*b*) They present a constant lithological aspect and consist of interbedded arenaceous and argillaceous rocks among which limestones are rare, conglomerates scarce and composed of small pebbles, breccias absent. The only variation in the assemblage appears in northern Sutherland, where hornblendic gneisses, possibly representing interbedded basic tuffs and lavas, make their appearance.

(*c*) The paragneisses of the Lewisian mainly represent an arenaceous series among which richly carbonaceous and calcareous sediments were abundant.

(*d*) The Torridonian sediments are dominantly arenaceous rocks. Basal breccias and conglomerates are abundant. The Torridonian assemblage shows very great variation in lithology and thickness in a N.-S. direction.

(*e*) Conglomerates of both the Moine Series and the Torridonian contain pebbles of quartzo-feldspathic granulite of Moine type.

(*f*) The Moine sediments were intruded, before their dynamothermal metamorphism, by many concordant and a few transgressive bodies mainly of basic composition. Intrusive rocks of similar composition appear in the Lewisian, but are unknown in the Scottish Torridonian.

(*g*) No trace of fossils has been found in Moine sediments in places where the original characters are sufficiently well-preserved to show depositional structures. Fossils, however, are uncommon in similar types of Palaeozoic sediment.

(*h*) Between the Moine Series and inliers of Lewisian orthogneiss and paragneiss dis-cordance, interpreted as unconformity, exists.

(*i*) No post-Lewisian, pre-Torridonian formation exists west of the zone of post-Cambrian thrust-movements.

(*k*) The Central Highland Granulites, which are equivalent to the Moine Series, are believed to be older than the Dalradian Schists. The age of the latter relative to the Cambro-Ordovician rocks of the Highland Border is unknown.

(*l*) The metamorphic grade of the Moine Schists is high, being equalled only, among British rocks of known age, in the Lewisian Gneiss.

(*m*) The Moine Series is said to resemble in degree of metamorphism and lithology the Seve Group of Scandinavia which is supposed to be a complex of Archaean and Silurian (*sensu lato*) rocks.

(*n*) A barrier, of land or sea impassable by neritic organisms, separated the Cambrian seas of the north-west region from the central (Highland Border) region of Scotland.

In view of stratigraphical discordance and lithological dissimilarity (items (*b*), (*c*) and (*h*)) the hypothesis that the Moine Series is of Lewisian age is not entertained here.

The hypothesis that the Series is a formation of post Lewisian but pre-Torridonian age has been widely accepted. It accounts for the discordance between Lewisian and Moine, and for the failure to find fossils. It is consistent with the interpretation of the Dalradian as a series older than the Cambro-Ordovician rocks of the Highland Border and probably younger than the Moine Schists, and defers to the disinclination of many geologists to regard so highly metamorphosed an assemblage as other than Archaean. Thus Horne visualized the Moine and Dalradian *schists* as forming a land barrier which separated the Cambrian seas of the north-west and central regions of Scotland. The hypothesis leaves unexplained the absence of a corresponding formation along the western seaboard and implies a pre-Torridonian period of orogeny along north-easterly lines and dynamothermal metamorphism of which no trace is preserved in the Lewisian Gneiss west of the post-Cambrian thrust-zone.

The view that the Moine Series is of Torridonian age was held by Peach and is indeed fashionable at the present day. This hypothesis necessitates the acceptance of a Caledonian age for the dynamothermal metamorphism of the Series. Certain of Peach's arguments are unsound, but his hypothesis accounts for the correspondence between the stratigraphical relations of the Moine Series and Torridonian to the Lewisian, for the fact that both Moine and Torridonian are shallow-water accumulations composed largely of feldspathic sandstone, and for the absence of any intermediate series in the Lewisian-Torridonian outcrop. Serious objections are: (i) the lack of proof that the metamorphism is of Caledonian age (*see* below); (ii) the infrequency of con-glomerates and the absence of breccias in the Moine Series; (iii) the contrast between the N. to S. variation in lithology and thickness of the Torridonian and the lithological constancy of the Moine assemblage in this direction; and (iv) the absence of intrusive sheets in the Torridonian. Clough suggested that lithological differences between the Moine Series and the Torridonian may be due to the fact that their strata were deposited in different areas. This suggestion accords with the writer's view that the Moine sediments are shallow sea or estuarine rather than flood-plain deposits like the Torridonian, and this distinction may explain the regional differences, as well as those of composition, between the two formations. For recent discussion of the age of Moines, Tarskavaig Moines, and Torridonian, papers by W. Q. Kennedy (1951), A. G. MacGregor (1952) and E. B. Bailey (1955) may be consulted.

The hypothesis that the Moine Series is of post-Cambrian age was accepted by many British geologists before the great thrust-planes of north-west Scotland were recognized. Since then this hypothesis has been advocated only by Frödin.

Age of the Dynamothermal Metamorphism. Three hypotheses have been advanced—namely, that the date of the metamorphism is: (i) Lewisian; (ii) post-Lewisian but pre-Torridonian; (iii) Caledonian—that is, Siluro-Devonian. A summary of the relevant facts and probabilities is given below.

(*a*) The isoclinal folding of the Moine Series on N.N.E.-S.S.W. axes was synchronous with the dynamothermal metamorphism of the sediments into schists (p. 30).

(*b*) The crystalline structure of the schists is broken down and their strike and dip affected by movement along the Moine Thrust-plane.

(*c*) Crystalline Moine schists are contact-altered by the Ben Loyal Syenite, an intrusion petrographically identical and probably coeval with the Loch Ailsh syenite which is sheared by the post-Cambrian thrust-movements.

(*d*) Minor intrusions into crystalline Moine schists are sheared by the thrust-movements.

(e) The Moine Series in Sutherland contains hornblendic, biotitic and pyroxenic gneisses and basic and ultrabasic minor intrusions ·which have been metamorphosed by the same regional processes as the contiguous schists.

(f) These gneisses and metamorphosed intrusions include rocks which are similar to, or even identical·with, types of gneiss and pre-Torridonian intrusions occurring in the Lewisian of the inliers and of parts of the western seaboard where pre-Torridonian earth-movements have effected modifications.

(g) Pebbles of metamorphic rocks indistinguishable from Moine granulite have been found, though rarely, in Torridonian strata.

(h) Pebbles of granulite resembling quartzo-feldspathic Moine granulite have been found in schistose conglomerate of the Moine Series (p. 35).

(i) It has been claimed that the Moine schists bordering the Moine Thrust-plane are less highly metamorphosed than the greater part of the Series.

(k) The Tarskavaig Moine rocks, which represent a more westerly part of the Series than the schists east of the Moine Thrust-plane, are less highly metamorphosed than the schists.

(l) Schistose grits, conglomeratic schist and phyllites with cataclastic structures occur about 18 miles east of the Moine Thrust-plane.

(m) Torridonian shales, dynamically altered in an intensely folded part of the post-Cambrian thrust-zone near Loch Carron, approximate in structure to crystalline schists.

Note on item (a). F. Coles Phillips maintains that the existing metamorphic condition of the schists was induced by compressive stresses acting along N.E.-S.W. lines and therefore probably of pre-Torridonian date (*see also* pp. 13 & 24).

Note on item (i). This claim has been disputed by Professor Read, who maintains that the appearance of comparatively low metamorphic grade is due to retrograde metamorphism associated with the post-Cambrian thrust-movements. Nevertheless, the geologists who made the claim had themselves recognized the retrograde effects as an item in the history of the schists distinct from and posterior to their dynamothermal metamorphism. The claim appears to be supported by recent work in Ardnamurchan and Moidart. The low grade of metamorphism is indicated by preservation of original structures and by fine crystalloblastic grain rather than by index metamorphic minerals. Garnet occurs even in the Tarskavaig Moine rocks.

A Lewisian age is suggested by Professor Read on the basis of the facts stated in items (b), (c), (e), and (f). This hypothesis necessarily involves acceptance of the Moine Schists as the equivalent of the Lewisian paragneisses and denial of the existence of inliers of Lewisian in the Moine Series. On p. 35 it has been pointed out that the Moine and Lewisian sediments are of different facies, while all geologists who have surveyed the inliers agree that discordance of some kind exists between them and the Moine Schists. Moreover, the resemblances noted in items (e) and (f) are petrographical resemblances only. The Lewisian members belong to a plutonic complex, the petrographically similar rocks in the Moine Series are basic igneous or pyroclastic rocks or sediments of peculiar composition interbanded with the ordinary Moine sediments. A Lewisian age for the metamorphism, and by corollary for the Series, therefore cannot be accepted.

The occurrence of pebbles of granulite of Moine type in Torridonian conglomerates was claimed by Gregory as proof of the pre-Torridonian age of the Series and of its dynamothermal metamorphism. The value of this evidence is doubtful since granulites of Moine type occur in conglomerates of the Moine Series.

The dynamothermal metamorphism is essentially connected with the crustal stresses which produced the N.N.E.-S.S.W. isoclinal folding of the Series. This folding has been considered, by many geologists, to be of Caledonian age. Objections which can be raised to this hypothesis are: (i) the folding is earlier than the thrust-movements by an interval sufficiently long to permit formation of the great granite-schist injection-complexes and intrusion of the alkaline masses of Sutherland; (ii) the strike of the folding is more northerly than the Caledonian folding in Southern Scotland; and (iii) the folding directly associated with the thrust-movements strikes N.W.-S.E. or W.N.W.-E.S.E. and is superimposed on the N.N.E.-S.S.W. folding (p. 24). On the other hand, it may be pointed out that the thrust-movements were probably comparatively late events in the Caledonian orogeny, since recrudescence of movement foliated minor intrusions of 'Newer Granite' age (p. 61), and that the strike of the main folding in the Moine Series is practically parallel to the strike of the post-Cambrian thrust-zone. Moreover, the thrust-fractures of the north-west and the intense folding of Southern Scotland furnish indisputable evidence that during the Caledonian period the Highland region was subjected to intense compression. As Clough suggested, the isoclinal folding of the Moine Series may represent the main, and the thrust-fractures the closing phase of Caledonian orogeny in the Northern Highlands. Analogy may be drawn with events in the south of Scotland where the stage of intense late Silurian folding was followed, after an interval of erosion and Lower Old Red Sandstone sedimentation and granitic intrusion, by powerful reversed faulting.

Peach regarded the metamorphism of the Torridonian in the thrust-zone and the metamorphism of the Moine Schists as differing only in degree. He considered, *see* items (*i*) and (*k*), that the metamorphic grade of the schists was lower in the west owing to smaller superincumbent load, and that the thrust-fractures also developed in this less heavily loaded region.

It seems to the writer that the balance of probability, with our still limited knowledge, is in favour of the view that the dynamothermal metamorphism of the Series is of early Caledonian age. If this conclusion is not accepted, then it becomes necessary to postulate a period of pre-Torridonian orogeny during which a system of folding was produced such as might have developed later during Caledonian times. (*See* Granite-Schist Injection-Complexes; General Remarks, p. 32, and Age, p. 33; *also* Kennedy 1948, 1949, 1955; MacGregor 1952; Bailey 1955).

REFERENCES
(*See also References on* p. 56)

1884. HEDDLE, M. F. The Geognosy and Mineralogy of Scotland—Sutherland. *Mineralogical Mag.*, vol. v, p. 71.
1885. LAPWORTH, C. On the Stratigraphy and Metamorphism of the Rocks of the Durness Eriboll District. *Proc. Geol. Assoc.*, vol. viii, p. 438.
1896. HORNE, J., and E. GREENLY. On Foliated Granites and their Relations to the Crystalline Schists in Eastern Sutherland. *Quart. Journ. Geol. Soc.*, vol. lii, p. 633.
1910. CLOUGH, C. T., C. B. CRAMPTON, and J. S. FLETT. The Augen Gneiss and Moine Sediments of Ross-shire. *Geol. Mag.*, vol. xlix, p. 344.
1915. GREGORY, J. W. Moine Pebbles in Torridonian Conglomerates. *Geol. Mag.*, vol. lvi, p. 447.
1922. FRÖDIN, G. On the Analogies between the Scottish and Scandinavian Portions of the Caledonian Mountain Range. *Bull. Geol. Inst. Univ. Upsala*, vol. xviii, p. 199.
1930. PEACH, B. N., and J. HORNE. *Chapters on the Geology of Scotland*. Oxford.
1934. BAILEY, E. B., and W. J. McCALLIEN. Pre-Cambrian Association. B. Second Excursion, Scotland. *Geol. Mag.*, vol. lxxi, p. 549.
1934. READ, H. H. Age Problems of the Moine Series. *Geol. Mag.*, vol. lxxi, p. 302.
1935. GREEN, J. F. N. The Moines. *Quart. Journ. Geol. Soc.*, vol. xci, p. lxiv.
1935. TILLEY, C. E. The rôle of kyanite in the 'hornfels zone' of the Càrn Chuinneag granite (Ross-shire). *Mineralogical Mag.*, vol. xxiv, p. 92.
1937. PHILLIPS, F. C. A Fabric Study of some Moine Schists and associated Rocks. *Quart. Journ. Geol. Soc.*, vol. xciii, p. 581.
1939. BAILEY, E. B. Caledonian Tectonics and Metamorphism in Skye. *Bull. Geol. Surv. Gt. Brit.*, No. 2, p. 46.
1939. PHILLIPS, F. C. Micro-frabric of some members of the 'Tarskavaig-Moine' Series. *Geol. Mag.*, vol. lxxvi, p. 229.

1939. RICHEY, J. E., and W. Q. KENNEDY. The Moine and Sub-Moine Series of Morar, Inverness-shire. *Bull. Geol. Survey Gt. Brit.*, No. 2, p. 26.
1939. DREVER, H. I. A Petrological Study of the Limestones in the Moine Series of Ardgour, Argyllshire. *Geol. Mag.*, vol. lxxvi, p. 501.
1940. DREVER, H. I. The Geology of Ardgour, Argyllshire. *Trans. Roy. Soc. Edin.*, vol. lx, p. 141.
1944. CHENG, YU-CHI. The Migmatite Area around Bettyhill, Sutherland. *Quart. Journ. Geol. Soc.*, vol. xcix, p. 107.
1945. PHILLIPS, F. C. The Micro-fabric of the Moine Schists. *Geol. Mag.*, vol. lxxxii, p. 205.
1946. CLOOS, E. Lineation. A critical Review and anotated Bibliography. *Mem. Geol. Soc. Amer.*, No. 18.
1948. ANDERSON, E. M. On lineation and petrofabric structure and the shearing movement by which they have been produced. *Quart. Journ. Geol. Soc.*, vol. civ, p. 99.
1948. HSING-YUAN, Ma. On the Occurrence of Agmatite in the Rogart Migmatite Area, Sutherland. A study in granitization. *Geol. Mag.*, vol. lxxxv, p. 1.
1948. KENNEDY, W. Q. The Significance of Thermal Structure in the Scottish Highlands. *Geol. Mag.*, vol. lxxxv, p. 229.
1948. WATSON, J. Late Sillimanite in the Migmatites of Kildonan, Sutherland. *Geol. Mag.*, vol. lxxxv, p. 149.
1948. MACGREGOR, A. G. Resemblances between Moine and 'Sub-Moine' Metamorphic Sediments in the Western Highlands of Scotland. *Geol. Mag.*, vol. lxxxv, p. 265.
1948. RICHEY, J. E. Pre-Metamorphism Cleavage in the Moine Schists of Morar, Western Inverness-shire. *Trans. Edin. Geol. Soc.*, vol. xiv, p. 200.
1949. KENNEDY, W. Q. Zones of Progressive Regional Metamorphism in the Moine Schists of the Western Highlands of Scotland. *Geol. Mag.*, vol. lxxxvi, p. 43.
1949. PHILLIPS, F. C. Lineation in Moinian and Lewisian Rocks of the Northern Highlands of Scotland. *Geol. Mag.*, vol. lxxxvi, p. 279.
1950. BAILEY, E. B. The Structural History of Scotland. *Rep. XVIIIth Internat. Geol. Congr.* (*Gt. Brit.*, 1948), pt. i, p. 230.
1951. CHARLU, T. G. K. A Note on the Development of Large Garnets in Sutherland Migmatites. *Geol. Mag.*, vol. lxxxviii, p. 185.
1951. PHILLIPS, F. C. Apparent Coincidences in the Life History of the Moine Schists. *Geol. Mag.*, vol. lxxxviii, p. 225.
1951. KENNEDY, W. Q. Sedimentary Differentiation as a Factor in the Moine Torridonian Correlation. *Geol. Mag.*, vol. lxxxviii, p. 257.
1951. MACGREGOR, A. G. Ice crystals in Glaciers compared with Quartz crystals in dynamically metamorphosed sandstones. *Journ. Glaciology*, vol. i, p. 564.
1952. BAILEY, E. B., and C. E. TILLEY. Rocks claimed as Conglomerate at the Moinian-Lewisian Junction. *Rep. of XVIIIth Internat. Geol. Congress* (*Gt. Brit.*, 1948), pt. xiii, p. 273.
1952. ANDERSON, E. M. Lineation and its Relation to Sub-crustal Convection Currents. *Geol. Mag.*, vol. lxxxix, p. 113.
1952. HOLTEDAHL, O. The structural history of Norway and its relation to Great Britain. *Quart. Journ. Geol. Soc.*, vol. cviii, p. 65.
1952. LEEDAL, G. P. The Cluanie igneous intrusion, Inverness-shire and Ross-shire. *Quart. Journ. Geol. Soc.*, vol. cviii, p. 35.
1952. MACGREGOR, A. G. Metamorphism in the Moine Nappe of Northern Scotland. *Trans. Edin. Geol. Soc.*, vol. xv, p. 241.
1952. MCINTYRE, D. B. The Tectonics of the Beinn Dronaig Area, Attadale. *Trans. Edin. Geol. Soc.*, vol. xv, p. 258.
1952. RUTLEDGE, H. The Structure of the Fannich Forest Pelitic Belt. *Trans. Edin. Geol. Soc.*, vol. xv, p. 317.
1952. WILSON, G. A Quartz Vein System in the Moine Series near Melness, A'Mhoine, North Sutherland, and its tectonic significance. *Geol. Mag.*, vol. lxxxix, p. 141.
1953. KVALE, A. Linear structures and their relation to movement in the Caledonides of Scandinavia and Scotland. *Quart. Journ. Geol. Soc.*, vol. cix, p. 51.
1953. MCLACHLAN, G. R. The Bearing of Rolled Garnets on the Concept of B-lineation in Moine Rocks. *Geol. Mag.*, vol. xc, p. 172.
1953. WILSON, G. Mullion and Rodding Structures in the Moine Series of Scotland. *Proc. Geol. Assoc.*, vol. lxiv, p. 118.
1953. WILSON, G., J. WATSON, and J. SUTTON. Current-bedding in the Moine Series of North-Western Scotland. *Geol. Mag.*, vol. xc, p. 377.
1953-59. MACGREGOR, A. G., and others. In *Sum. Prog. Geol. Surv.*, for 1951, p. 44; for 1952, p. 36; for 1953, p. 48; for 1954, p. 48; for 1955, p. 48; for 1956, p. 45; for 1957, p. 41; for 1958, p. 43.
1954. BAILEY, E. B. Relations of Torridonian to Durness Limestone in the Broadford-Strollamus district of Skye. *Geol. Mag.*, vol. xci, p. 73.
1954. CHRISTIE, J. M., D. B. MCINTYRE, and L. E. WEISS. Appendix to paper by D. B. McIntyre. *Proc. Geol. Assoc.*, vol. lxv, p. 219.

1954a. HARKER, R. I. The Occurrence of Orthoclase and Microcline in the Granitic Gneisses of the Càrn Chuinneag—Inchbae Complex, E. Ross-shire. *Geol. Mag.*, vol. xci, p. 129.

1954b. HARKER, R. I. Further Data on the Petrology of the Pelitic Hornfelses of the Càrn Chuinneag—Inchbae Region, Ross-shire. *Geol. Mag.*, vol. xci, p. 445.

1954. HARRY, W. T. The composite granite gneiss of Western Ardgour, Argyll. *Quart. Journ. Geol. Soc.*, vol. cix for 1953, p. 285.

1954. MCINTYRE, D. B. The Moine Thrust—its discovery, age and tectonic significance. *Proc. Geol. Assoc.*, vol. lxv, p. 203.

1954. SUTTON, J., and J. WATSON. The structure and stratigraphical succession of the Moines of Fannich Forest and Strath Bran. *Quart. Journ. Geol. Soc.*, vol. cx, p. 21.

1955. BAILEY, E. B. Moine Tectonics and Metamorphism in Skye. *Trans. Edin. Geol. Soc.*, vol. xvi, p. 93.

1955. KENNEDY, W. Q. The tectonics of the Morar Anticline and the problem of the North-West Caledonian Front. *Quart. Journ. Geol. Soc.*, vol. cx for 1954, p. 357.

1956. CRAMPTON, C. B. Loch Shin Limestone: Comparison of Dolomite and Calcite Fabrics. *Trans. Edin. Geol. Soc.*, vol. xvi, p. 334.

1956. HARKER, R. I. The Stratigraphy and Folding of some Metamorphosed Moine Sediments around the Càrn Chuinneag and Inchbae Granitic Gneisses. *Geol. Mag.*, vol. xciii, p. 57.

1956. HARLAND, W. B. Tectonic Facies, Orientation, Sequence, Style and Date. *Geol. Mag.*, vol. xciii, p. 111.

1956. JOHNSON, M. R. W. Conjugate fold systems in the Moine Thrust Zone in the Loch Carron and Coulin Forest areas of Wester Ross. *Geol. Mag.*, vol. xciii, p. 345.

1956. RAMSAY, J. G. The supposed Moinian Basal Conglomerate at Glen Strathfarrar Inverness-shire. *Geol. Mag.*, vol. xciii, p. 32.

1956. READ, H. H. The Last Twenty Years' Work in the Moine Series of Scotland. *Verh. Ned. Geol.-mijnb. Genoot.*, vol. xvi.

1957. CLIFFORD, P., M. J. FLEUTY, J. G. RAMSAY, J. SUTTON, and J. WATSON. The Development of Lineation in Complex Fold Systems. *Geol. Mag.*, vol. xciv, p. 1.

1957. CLIFFORD, T. N. The stratigraphy and structure of part of the Kintail district of southern Ross-shire: its relation to the Northern Highlands. *Quart. Journ. Geol. Soc.*, vol. cxiii, p. 57.

1957. CRAMPTON, C. B. Regional Study of Epidote, Mica and Albite Fabrics of the Moines. *Geol. Mag.*, vol. xciv, p. 89.

1957. JOHNSON, M. R. W. The Structural Geology of the Moine Thrust Zone in the Coulin Forest, Wester Ross. *Quart. Journ. Geol. Soc.*, vol. cxiii, p. 241.

1958. CHRISTIE, J. M. Dynamic Interpretation of the Fabric of a Dolomite from the Moine Thrust Zone in North-west Scotland. *Amer. Journ. Sci.*, vol. cclvi, p. 159.

1958a. CRAMPTON, C. B. Muscovite, Biotite and Quartz Fabric Reorientation. *Journ. Geol.*, vol. lxvi, p. 28.

1958b. CRAMPTON, C. B. Structural Petrology of Cambro-Ordovician Limestones of the North-west Highlands of Scotland. *Amer. Journ. Sci.*, vol. cclvi p. 145.

1958. CLIFFORD, T. N. A note on Kyanite in the Moine Series of Southern Ross-shire and a review of related rocks in the Northern Highlands of Scotland. *Geol. Mag.*, vol. xcv, p. 333.

1958. FRANCIS, G. H. The Amphibolite of Doir' a' Chatha (Durcha) Sutherland. *Geol. Mag.*, vol. xcv, p. 25.

1958. HARLAND, W. B., and M. B. BAYLY. Tectonic Regimes. *Geol. Mag.*, vol. xcv, p. 89.

1958. LAMBERT, R. St J. A Metamorphic Boundary in the Moine Schists of the Morar and Knoydart Districts of Inverness-shire. *Geol. Mag.*, vol. xcv, p. 177.

1958a. RAMSAY, J. G. Superimposed folding at Loch Morar, Inverness-shire and Ross-shire. *Quart. Journ. Geol. Soc.*, vol. cxiii for 1957, p. 271.

1958b. RAMSAY, J. G. Moine-Lewisian relations at Glenelg, Inverness-shire. *Quart. Journ. Geol. Soc.*, vol. cxiii for 1957, p. 487.

1959. CLIFFORD, P. The Geological Structure of the Loch Luichart Area, Ross-shire. *Circ. Geol. Soc. Lond.*, No. 73.

1959. CRAMPTON, C. B. Fabric Analysis of Moine and Cambrian Quartzites of the North-west Highlands of Scotland. *Proc. Geol. Soc. Lond.*, No. 1566, p. 33.

1959. LAMBERT, R. St J. Progressive and Retrogressive Metamorphism in the Morar and Knoydart Districts of Inverness-shire. *Trans. Roy. Soc. Edin.*, vol. lxiii, pt. iii, p. 553.

1959. SUTTON, J., and J. WATSON. Structures in the Caledonides between Loch Duich and Glenelg, North-West Highlands. *Quart. Journ. Geol. Soc.*, vol. cxiv for 1958, p. 231.

The Geological Survey Memoirs listed on pp. 103,104 form an important part of the literature on the Moine Series.

IV. TORRIDONIAN

STRATA of this age rest unconformably on an old land-surface of Lewisian Gneiss (Plate IIIb). In the north-west of Sutherland this surface was gently undulating but from Quinag southwards showed irregular and locally high relief. Striking examples of the old Archaean hills are to be seen at Quinag and Slioch (Fig. 10 and Plate I), where Torridon sandstones abut against hills of gneiss still rising 1,200 ft and 2,000 ft respectively above the general level of the gneiss surface. Valleys in this ancient land-surface, though now occupied by Torridon Sandstone, can still be traced and the present drainage in the south of Assynt and to the north-east of Loch Maree follows lines established in the far distant past.

The various rocks of the Torridonian are practically unaltered. The feldspathic sandstones and grits (arkoses) retain their original structure and show both brown and white clastic mica. Current-bedding is conspicuous. Shales though indurated do not possess a true cleavage and in many places rain-pittings, sun-cracks, and ripple-marks are well preserved. Equally remarkable is the absence of strong folding in the Torridonian strata west of the thrust-zone. Dips are often very low, but since the overlying Cambrian sediments are inclined at 10 to 20 degrees in an easterly direction, it is apparent that the Torridon Sandstone had been tilted downwards to the west by a corresponding amount in pre-Cambrian times. Powerful faults throwing from one to several thousand feet are fairly common; the direction is generally north-east to north, but important dislocations trending north-west also occur. Studies have been made of Torridonian palaeomagnetism (Irving and Runcorn 1957). The direction of magnetization, which is due to alignment of haematite grains during deposition of the sediments, is believed to have remained substantially unaltered since sedimentation; it is directed N.W.-S.E. being N.W. positive in the Diabaig but reversing to N.W. negative in the Applecross and Aultbea groups, the reversal taking place within but near the top of the Diabaig.

No recognizable fossil remains have been found. Evidence of life is preserved only in obscure worm-tracks in carbonaceous shales of the Diabaig group and in phosphatic concretions in shales of the Aultbea—the highest—group. The brown amorphous phosphate contains minute spherical bodies and brown fibres. Cupriferous nodules occur in Diabaig shales at Clachtoll, Sutherland (Fermor 1951).

The major subdivisions of the Torridonian are shown in the first table on p. 44 and their distribution in Fig. 11.

The variable thickness of the groups is, in part, a consequence of the irregularity of the Lewisian land-surface, but must also be due to overlap and decrease in sedimentation from south to north. It is noteworthy that the Diabaig group is represented at Stoer and in the thrust-belt at Conival but is absent in the intervening ground.

The *Diabaig sediments of Skye* have been subdivided as shown in the second table on p. 44 and it is of interest to remember that these strata all lie within the thrust-belt.

The lowest sub-group contains clastic epidote and pebbles of epidosite and epidotic gneiss derived from the old land-surface. The green colour of some of the beds is due to chlorite. Bands rich in magnetite and other heavy minerals

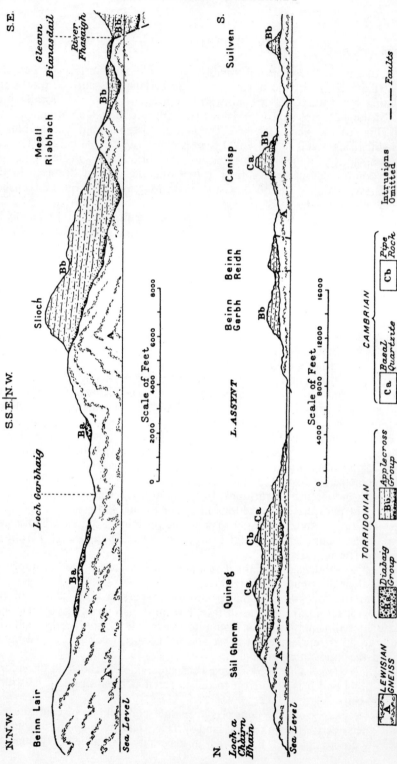

FIG. 10. *Sections illustrating the unconformity of Torridon Sandstone on Lewisian Gneiss.*

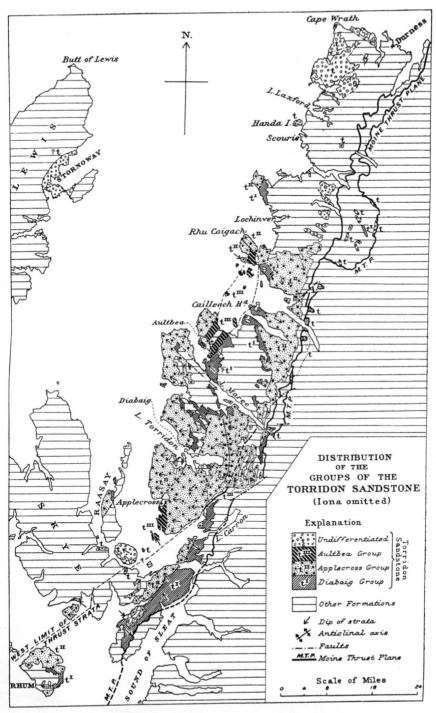

FIG. 11. *Distribution of the groups of the Torridon Sandstone.*

occur in the Kinloch Beds and in the Applecross Group. Breccias which form the local base of the Diabaig and Applecross groups are composed of Lewisian Gneiss of the neighbourhood and can be traced for short distances only. In the layers of more waterworn conglomeratic material in the Applecross grits the pebbles offer a remarkable lithological contrast to those of the breccias. They are composed largely of rocks which are not known in place and consist mainly

	APPROXIMATE THICKNESS IN FEET	LITHOLOGY (MAINLAND)
AULTBEA GROUP	3,000 to 4,500 in Coigach; 250 at Cape Wrath	Sandstones, flags, dark and black shales and calcareous bands passing down into chocolate and red sandstones, and grey micaceous flags with partings of grey and green shale.
APPLECROSS GROUP ..	6,000 to 8,000 in Applecross; 1,000 at Cape Wrath	Chocolate and red arkoses, with conglomeratic layers. Occasional chocolate and red shales. Local basement breccias.
DIABAIG GROUP ..	Absent in the north; 500 in Gairloch; 7,200 in Skye	Hard, fine red sandstones at top, red and dark mudstones, dark grey sandy shales with calcareous lenticles. At base breccias and boulder beds of local origin.

of vein quartz, quartzite, chert, and jasper with important percentages of grit, felsite and feldspar-porphyry, while schistose and metamorphic rocks are rare. Sir J. J. H. Teall directed special attention to the presence of pebbles of spherulitic felsite identical with the felsite of the Uriconian Series of Shropshire. The arkoses are likewise peculiar in that the dominant feldspars are microcline and microcline-microperthite, though these species are not abundant in the Lewisian Gneiss except in the north where granite intrusions are numerous. E. B. Bailey (1955) has given a detailed account of the Skye Torridonian.

In *Iona* strata regarded as Torridonian include an older group consisting of dark grey and dark green grits with a basal conglomerate and containing some thick bands of shale in the upper part, together with a younger group of flags characterized by rapid alternations of sandy and shaly material. The conglomerate is intensely sheared and the grits are to a small extent epidotic. The

DIABAIG GROUP (SKYE)	THICKNESS	LITHOLOGY
KINLOCH BEDS ..	3,600 ft	Dark grey sandy shales, fine-grained grey and buff grits with thin calcareous lenticles.
BEINN NA SEAMRAIG GRITS	2,600 „	Fine-grained grits, bands of grey, sandy shales.
LOCH NA DAL BEDS ..	600 to 1,200 ft	Dark grey sandy shales, fine-grained grits and small calcareous lenticles.
EPIDOTIC GRITS ..	200 to 300 „	Green and yellow grits and conglomerates. Occasional purple or purple and green shales.

pebbles in the conglomerate are mainly acid igneous rock, with hornblendic rock and quartz in places, while jasper, aplite, red soda-granite, and nordmarkite have also been noted. The strata are almost unaltered, except for the intense crushing of the basal conglomerate, and are only rarely cleaved. Isoclinal folding is believed to be present, but the thickness of the strata exposed on the island is estimated as about 2,000 ft. On some small islands off the south-east coast of Iona biotite and andalusite-hornfelses have been produced by contact-alteration of Torridonian shales by the Ross of Mull Granite.

Outer Hebrides. Near Stornoway a conglomerate with lenticular layers of soft, chocolate-coloured sandstone outcrops over about 10 sq miles, and rests unconformably on Lewisian Gneiss. The thickness is estimated as at least 9,000 ft. The boulders in it include sheared gneiss and are all of local origin. In this respect they differ from the Torridonian conglomerates of the mainland, and further differences lie in the decomposed condition of the feldspar and the comparatively low degree of induration in the deposits. The age is therefore uncertain. Jehu and Craig (1934) and Steavenson regard these strata as Torridonian, but Stevens refers them to the Trias, and Kürsten to the Old Red Sandstone.

Conditions of deposition. Persistent false-bedding, concentration of heavy minerals, occurrence of ripple-marks, sun-cracks, and rain-pits, show that the Torridonian strata accumulated in shallow water, subject at times to strong current action and at times liable to recession. Northerly overlap of higher over lower strata and constant south-easterly dip of the current-bedding indicate that the mainland lay towards the north or north-west. During Diabaig times, however, that part of the northern Highlands between Durness and Loch Maree remained dry land and was gradually buried during the period of deposition of the Applecross sediments. This area contributed only scree and hill-wash to form local deposits of breccia in the Torridonian succession. From the land to the north-west, materials of different type were derived, and the wind-faceted surfaces of many of the pebbles together with the remarkable freshness of the feldspar grains suggest that this land was or had been desert.

REFERENCES

1819. MACCULLOCH, J. *A Description of the Western Islands of Scotland.* Edinburgh.
1857. NICOL, J. On the Red Sandstone and Conglomerate and the Superposed Quartz-rocks, Limestone, and Gneiss of the North-west Coast of Scotland. *Quart. Journ. Geol. Soc.,* vol. xiii, p. 17.
1861. MURCHISON, R. I., and A. GEIKIE. On the Altered Rocks of the Western Islands of Scotland and the North-western and Central Highlands. *Quart. Journ. Geol. Soc.,* vol. xvii, p. 171.
1880. GEIKIE, Sir A. A Fragment of Primeval Europe. *Nature,* vol. xxii, p. 407.
1914. STEVENS, A. Notes on the Geology of the Stornoway District of Lewis. *Trans. Geol. Soc. Glasgow,* vol. xv, 1914, p. 51.
1915. GREGORY, J. W. Moine Pebbles in the Torridonian Conglomerates. *Geol. Mag.,* dec. vi, vol. ii, p. 447.
1922. JEHU, T. J. The Archaean and Torridonian Formations and the later Intrusive Rocks of Iona. *Trans. Roy. Soc. Edin.,* vol. liii, p. 165.
1928. DOUGAL, J. WILSON. Observations on the Geology of Lewis. *Trans. Edin. Geol. Soc.,* vol. xii, pt. i, p. 16.
1928. STEAVENSON, A. G. Some Geological Notes on Three Districts of Northern Scotland. *Trans. Geol. Soc. Glasgow,* vol. xviii, pt. i, p. 193, with note by M. Macgregor, p. 202.
1930. PEACH, B. N., and J. HORNE. *Chapters in the Geology of Scotland.* Oxford.
1934. JEHU, T. J., and R. M. CRAIG. Geology of the Outer Hebrides; Part V. *Trans. Roy. Soc. Edin.,* vol. lvii, p. 839.

1951. FERMOR, L. L. On a Discovery of Copper-ore in the Torridonian Rocks of Sutherland. *Geol. Mag.*, vol. lxxxviii, p. 215.

1951. KENNEDY, W. Q. Sedimentary Differentiation as a Factor in the Moine-Torridonian Correlation. *Geol. Mag.*, vol. lxxxviii, p. 257.

1954. BAILEY, E. B. Relations of Torridonian to Durness Limestone in the Broadford-Strollamus district of Skye. *Geol. Mag.*, vol. xci, p. 73.

1955. BAILEY, E. B. Moine Tectonics and Metamorphism in Skye. *Trans. Edin. Geol. Soc.*, vol. xvi, p. 93.

1957. IRVING, E. The Origin of the Palaeomagnetism of the Torridonian Sandstone of North-west Scotland. *Phil. Trans. Roy. Soc. Lond.* A, vol. ccl, p. 100.

1957. IRVING, E., and S. K. RUNCORN. Analysis of the Palaeomagnetism of the Torridonian Sandstone Series of North-west Scotland. *Phil. Trans. Roy. Soc. Lond.* A, vol. ccl, p. 83.

1957. KÜRSTEN, M. The Metamorphic and Tectonic History of Parts of the Outer Hebrides. *Trans. Edin. Geol. Soc.*, vol. xvii, p. 1.

See also Geological Survey Memoirs (pp. 103,104) on North-west Highlands, Iona, Small Isles, Glenelg, Central Ross-shire and Fannich Mountains.

V. CAMBRIAN AND EARLY ORDOVICIAN

AFTER the deposition of the Torridonian a period of crustal warping and vigorous erosion ensued. The Torridonian was in places completely removed and the underlying gneiss itself attacked by the agencies of denudation. Eventually a plane of marine denudation was produced and on this surface the Cambrian strata were deposited. The basal Cambrian sediments therefore transgress bed after bed of the Torridonian until they cross the surface of unconformity between the Torridonian and Lewisian, and thereafter rest on the gneiss (Plate I). The crossing of the lower surface of unconformity by the upper is displayed with great clarity in Assynt (Fig. 12).

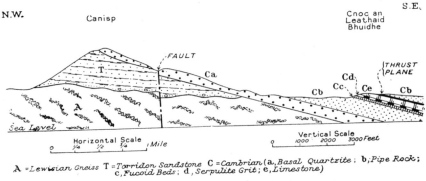

FIG. 12. *Section illustrating the unconformity of Cambrian strata on Torridon Sandstone and Lewisian Gneiss.*

The distribution of Cambrian and early Ordovician sediments is shown in Plate II. They outcrop in normal sequence along a narrow belt which stretches from Loch Kishorn to Loch Eireboll and in faulted outliers at Achiltibuie and Durness. The strata dip generally towards the east-south-east at angles varying between 5 and 20 degrees. East of the long belt, Cambrian strata enter largely into the zone of thrust-masses, in which they may lie at any angle and are sometimes inverted. The Cambrian and early Ordovician strata of Skye probably all lie within the thrust-zone.

In Fig. 13 the divisions and groups, the lithology and palaeontology of the Cambrian and early Ordovician of North-west Scotland are summarized. The thicknesses of the groups are generalized and, in the case of the Durness Limestone, are only approximate.

The **Arenaceous Series** is topographically the most prominent member. At the base a thin conglomerate, 1 to 10 ft thick, contains pebbles of pink and white quartz, feldspar, jasper, quartzite, and felsite. Only at one locality have fossil remains, worm-casts, been found in the Basal Quartzite. The upper group, however, is remarkable for the abundance of the vertical cylinders, or 'pipes', which represent the casts of worm-burrows (*Scolithus linearis*). The pipes are of various kinds and it has been found possible to divide the piped quartzite into five zones distinguished by difference in type and abundance of the pipes.

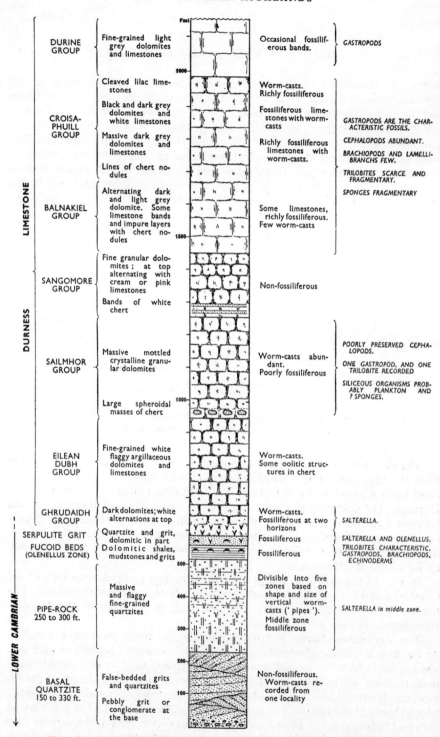

FIG. 13. *Vertical section of the Cambrian and Early Ordovician.*

The laminations of flaggy beds are bent down and attenuated around the pipes, and cup-like depressions exist at the upper ends. These peculiarities and the succession of zones have proved of value in determining, within areas involved in thrust-movements, whether the strata are in the normal position or inverted. The thickness of the Basal Quartzite varies between 150 (Sutherland) and 330 ft (Skye), that of the Pipe-Rock between 250 and 300 ft.

Passage or **Middle Series.** The lower group consists of dolomitic shales and mudstones, 40 to 50 ft thick, on the bedding-planes of which flattened worm-casts (*Planolites*) are abundant. Originally interpreted as fucoid markings, these have given the name '*Fucoid Beds*' to this group. Shales near the middle of the Fucoid Beds have yielded a fossil assemblage almost identical with that of the *Olenellus* Zone of North America. Trilobites, *e.g. Olenellus lapworthi, O. reticulatus, Olenelloides armatus*, are the diagnostic fossils, and the fauna includes also a few brachiopods and the molluscs *Salterella* and *Hyolithes*.

The upper group consists of a thin but very persistent grit, 30 ft thick. At the base the grit is interleaved with shales from which *Olenellus* has been obtained, and at the top becomes dolomitic and carious-weathering. Seams of the dolomitic grit are charged with *Salterella*. The original description of this fossil as *Serpulites maccullochi* caused the name '*Serpulite Grit*' to be attached to the group.

Calcareous Series or **Durness Limestone.** The lithological sub-division of the succession at Durness is shown in Fig. 13. The three lower groups have been definitely recognized in Skye, but the Sangomore group only doubtfully. The higher groups in Skye have local names, the Beinn an Dubhaich, Strath Suardal, and Ben Suardal groups. The latter has yielded a rich fauna which shows that it is probably homotaxial with the Croisaphuill and Balnakiel groups of Durness. The Strath Suardal limestone contains chert lumps, an inch or two across, which resemble sponges in shape but do not show any clear organic structure. Similar spheroidal or ovoid forms in the Beinn an Dubhaich limestone, which is contact-altered by Tertiary granophyre, are composed of concentric zones of serpentine and carbonate and resemble *Eozoon canadense*.

The lowest 30 feet of the Ghrudaidh limestone has yielded *Salterella* and is therefore regarded as Lower Cambrian. This fossil has also been found by M. Macgregor and the writer in white limestone which was mapped by Peach as Eilean Dubh. The Lower Cambrian may therefore embrace a larger portion of the Durness Limestone than has hitherto been suspected. At Balnakiel three algal bands have been found by Dr. V. Wilson at horizons about 255, 270, and 320 ft above the base of the Eilean Dubh group, which is here 440 ft thick, according to Dr. Wilson's observations. The next fossil horizon occurs in the Sailmhor group and has yielded a few gastropods and cephalopods and a doubtful asaphoid trilobite. The assemblage is not diagnostic but some writers have inferred an Upper Cambrian age; others, for instance C. Poulsen, prefer to assign an Ordovician age to this fauna. The period of the Middle and perhaps also of the Upper Cambrian must therefore be represented by barren sediment of trifling thickness, unless an unconformity intervenes. Grabau suggested that a thin breccia within the Eilean Dubh group on Eilean Dubh, Durness, is important in this connection, but Peach and Horne considered it of only local significance.

In the Balnakiel and Croisaphuill groups the limestones yield a rich molluscan fauna which consists mainly of gastropods and cephalopods, including *Maclurea acuminata, Hormotoma [Murchisonia] antiqua, H. dubia, Lecanospira [Ophileta] compacta, Trochonema* ? *[Oriostoma] calphurnia, Euconia thule, Helicotoma spinosa; Protocycloceras [Actinoceras] mendax, Piloceras invaginatum, Endoceras spp.* Dr. V. Wilson has observed an algal band 36 ft above the base of the Balnakiel group. There are also recorded a few brachiopods, carapaces of the crustacean *Euchasma blumenbachi,* several trilobites including *Petigurus [Bathyurus] nero,* and a sponge *Archaeoscyphia.* This assemblage is almost identical with that of the Beekmantown Limestone of Pennsylvania and Newfoundland, which is regarded by most American geologists as Lower Ordovician but is referred by Ulrich and Schuchert to the Canadian—a formation extending from Upper Cambrian to Lower Ordovician. B. N. Peach (1913), on the grounds that there is commingling of Ordovician and Cambrian faunas in the Beekmantown beds, and that the latter were overlain by shales containing Arenig graptolites, maintained the position that the Croisaphuill and Balnakiel horizons belong to the Upper Cambrian, in accordance with British classification. Nevertheless, in Fig. 27, *Chapters on the Geology of Scotland* (1931). Peach and Horne indicate the top of the Durness Limestone as Ordovician. C. Poulsen (1951) has correlated the Sailmhor to Croisaphuill groups with the Cape Weber Formation of East Greenland which he regards as Ordovician in age; the highest group of the Durness sequence, the Durine Group which is poorly fossiliferous, he has referred with doubt to the Llanvirn.

The Durness Limestone represents very fine calcareous mud which accumulated so slowly that the fossils were partially dissolved before being covered up. The layers and nodules of chert are probably due to redeposition of silica derived from solution of siliceous organisms. Sponge spicules have been observed in some of the cherts. The abundant dolomites of the series were regarded by Peach as due to contemporaneous dolomitization. He suggested also that the magnesian salts of minute marine plants might have been concentrated by selective solution of their calcareous matter.

REFERENCES

1814. MACCULLOCH, J. *A Description of the Western Islands of Scotland.* 3 vols. Edinburgh.
1814. MACCULLOCH, J. Remarks on Several Parts of Scotland which exhibit Quartz Rock. *Trans. Geol. Soc.,* ser. i, vol. 2, p. 450.
1855. PEACH, C. W. Notice of the Discovery of Fossils in the Limestones of Durness, in the County of Sutherland. *Edin. New. Phil. Journ.* (n.s.), vol. ii, p. 197.
1857. NICOL, J. On the Old Red Sandstone and Conglomerate and the Superposed Quartzrocks, etc. *Quart. Journ. Geol. Soc.,* vol. xiii, p. 17.
1858. MURCHISON, R. I. The Quartz-rocks, Crystalline Limestone, and Micaceous Schists of the North-West Highlands of Scotland . . . with a Note on the Fossils by J. W. Salter. *Rep. Brit. Assoc.,* for 1857, p. 82.
1858. PEACH, C. W. Notice of the Discovery of Fossils in the Limestone of Durness, in the County of Sutherland. *Proc. Roy. Phys. Soc. Edin.,* vol. i, p. 23.
1859. MURCHISON, R. I. On the Succession of the Older Rocks in the northernmost Counties of Scotland, with some Observations on the Orkney and Shetland Islands. *Quart. Journ. Geol. Soc.,* vol. xv, p. 353.
1859. SALTER, J. W. Durness Limestone Fossils Described. *Quart. Journ. Geol. Soc.,* vol. xv. p. 374.
1888. GEIKIE, Sir A. On the Age of the Altered Limestone of Strath, Skye. *Quart. Journ. Geol. Soc.,* vol. xliv, p. 62.
1888. LAPWORTH, C. On the Discovery of the Olenellus Fauna in the Lower Cambrian Rocks of Britain. *Geol. Mag.,* new ser., dec. 3, vol. v, p. 484.
1892. PEACH, B. N., and J. HORNE. The Olenellus Zone in the North-West Highlands of Scotland. *Quart. Journ. Geol. Soc.,* vol. xlviii, p. 227.

1894. PEACH, B. N. Additions to the Fauna of the Olenellus Zone of the North-West High-
    lands. *Quart. Journ. Geol. Soc.*, vol. 1, p. 661.
1901. HORNE, J. Recent Advances in Scottish Geology. *Rep. Brit. Assoc.*, p. 615.
1901. PEACH, B. N. The Cambrian Fossils of the North-West Highlands. *Rep. Brit. Assoc.*,
    p. 642.
1913. PEACH, B. N. The Relation between the Cambrian Faunas of Scotland and North
    America. *Rep. Brit. Assoc.*, p. 448.
1916. GRABAU, A. W. Comparison of American and European Lower Ordovicic Formations.
    Bull. Geol. Soc. Amer., vol. xxvii, p. 562.
1929. ULRICH, E. O. Ordovician Trilobites of the Family Telephidae and Concerned Strati-
    graphical Correlations. *Proc. U.S. Nat. Mus.*, vol. lxxvi, Art. 21, p. 83.
1930. PEACH, B. N., and J. HORNE. *Chapters on the Geology of Scotland.* Oxford.
1936. JONES, O. T. The Lower Palaeozoic Rocks of Britain. *Rep. of XVIth Intern. Geol.
    Congress* (Washington, 1933), p. 463 and p. 467.
1951. POULSEN, C. The position of the East Greenland Cambro-Ordovician in the Palaeo-
    geography of the North Atlantic Region. *Medd. Dansk Geol. Foren.*, Bd. 12.
1951. MACGREGOR, M. Lapworth and the North-West Highlands succession. In symposium
    'The work of Charles Lapworth'. *Advanc. Sci.*, vol. vii, No. 28, p. 440.
1956. STUBBLEFIELD, C. J. Cambrian Palaeogeography in Britain (El Sistema Cambrico, su
    Palaeografia y el Problema de su Base: Symposium, vol. 1, pp. 1-43), edited by
    J. Rodgers, *XXth Internat. Geol. Congress*, Mexico, 1956.
  See also Geological Survey Memoirs (p. 103) on North-west Highlands, Glenelg, Central
    Ross-shire and Fannich Mountains, and vols. xxxv, xxxvi, and xxxvii of the Special
    Reports on the Mineral Resources of Great Britain (p. 104).

VI. POST-CAMBRIAN INTRUSIONS IN ASSYNT

Sills and Dykes. The Cambrian of Assynt is intruded by an extensive suite of sills of felsite, porphyrite, and hornblende-lamprophyre. Felsite and porphyrite sheets also follow the bedding of the Torridon Sandstone and the foliation of the Lewisian Gneiss, and a few similar dykes cut the latter. These intrusions outcrop very largely within the thrust-zone and are often highly sheared. The acid porphyrite known as Canisp Porphyry forms thick sheets in the Torridonian and dykes in the gneiss west of the thrust-zone. Greatly sheared sills of nordmarkite-porphyry appear in the Moine Schists close above the Moine Thrust-plane. In the direction parallel to the thrust-zone this hypabyssal suite has an extension of 18 miles in Assynt and reappears at Ullapool 12 miles farther south. Transverse to this direction the sills outcrop over a stretch of 13 miles, but dykes still occur 6 miles farther west. Allowing for a reduction in their east-west extension of at least 10 miles on account of thrust-movement, there appears some reason to believe that the original distribution was symmetrical around the Loch Borrolan laccolith (*see* Fig. 16, p. 62).

Petrographically the rocks show continuous variation from felsite through acid and hornblendic porphyrite to vogesite or spessartite, and the suite has a distinct resemblance to the Lower Old Red Sandstone intrusions of Central Scotland. It is, however, somewhat more sodic as shown by chemical analysis and by the appearance of aegirine in the more acid members. A vogesite sill near Inchnadamff has almost the same composition as the Loch Ailsh shonkinite (*see also* p. 53). Recently P. A. Sabine (1953) has made a comprehensive study of the post-Cambrian minor intrusions. He has shown that the distribution of the rock-types is related to the geological formation into which they are intruded and can therefore be used in structural interpretation.

Laccoliths. The *Loch Borrolan* laccolith, 10 square miles in extent, is intrusive in Cambrian strata within the lowermost nappe in Assynt. It is composed of quartz-syenite, leucocratic and mesocratic nepheline-syenites, and ultrabasic rocks, and of these components the first bulks largest. The mass has apparently a layered arrangement, the higher layers being successively richer in silica and poorer in dark minerals, and Shand explained this structure as due to gravitative differentiation in place probably after assimilation of limestone. There is, however, evidence that the ultrabasic part is intrusive into quartzite; the junction between leucocratic and mesocratic components is sharp and possibly vertical, and there is no field evidence of assimilation. Moreover, dykes of melanite-nepheline-syenite identical with the mesocratic component are found intrusive in Torridon Sandstone in Coigach, 20 miles west of Loch Borrolan. The writer therefore believes that the differentiation was complete before emplacement and that the structure of the mass is due to successive intrusion (*see also* Sabine 1953).

Melanite is the characteristic dark mineral and occurs in all the components, though in parts its place is taken by pyroxene. The ultrabasic rocks include melanite- and hornblende-pyroxenites. Among the nepheline-syenites, borolanite, a mesocratic type which carries conspicuous white spots, is well known. The spots are composed of orthoclase and altered nepheline and are perhaps pseudomorphs after leucite, but they pass into pegmatitic veins and segregations. Certain features of this part of the mass suggest that it is composite of meso-cratic syenite and later pegmatitic syenite.

The mass contains late dyke-like segregations of fresh nepheline- and sodalite-syenite and several definite dykes of aegirine-microgranite. Sulphatic cancrinite has been recorded by F. H. Stewart as a major constituent of the pegmatitic patches and veins in borolanite. C. E. Tilley has given additional chemical and petrological data on the alkaline rocks of Assynt; he has shown that the mineral regarded as sodalite by Shand in the dyke-rock to which he gave the name 'assyntite' is in fact nosean.

The *Loch Ailsh* laccolith, 5 sq miles in area, lies on a minor thrust-plane within the Ben More nappe. It also is arranged in layers of downwardly increasing specific gravity, but the structure is due to successive intrusion of ultrabasic followed by mesocratic and later by leucocratic rock. The floor lies in quartzite and the roof in limestone. Along the northern margin the con-cordant nature of the mass is revealed by large xenoliths of Cambrian strata dipping into the igneous rock in their proper stratigraphical order. The rocks of this mass differ from those of Loch Borrolan in that albite takes the place of nepheline, while quartz and melanite are both of subordinate importance. That is, the Loch Ailsh mass represents a magma in which scarcely any silica-differentiation has taken place and therefore quartz-syenite and nepheline-syenite are rare or absent, whereas in the Loch Borrolan mass silica-differentia-tion has been so extreme that only a very small quantity of simple syenite remains, while quartz-syenite and nepheline-syenite are both abundant.

The main rock of the Loch Ailsh mass is syenite in which albite bulks twice as largely as orthoclase and dark minerals are practically absent. Aegirine-augite- and riebeckite-syenites are less abundant. Shonkinite forms the meso-cratic, and biotite- and hornblende-pyroxenites the melanocratic zone. Dykes of aegirine-felsite cut the mass and also the adjacent quartzite and gneiss.

Contact-metamorphism. Both laccoliths contact-alter the Cambrian sediments. The dolomitic limestones are converted to diopside-, forsterite-, tremolite- and brucite-marbles, and occasionally to wollastonite-rock. To a very limited extent there has been interaction between the igneous rock and the dolomite, and 'skarn' rocks carrying zoisite, idocrase, and grossular have been formed. By introduction of potash from the syenite mica-diopside-, mica-tremolite- and mica-rocks have been developed from dolomite.

Age. The intrusions considered above may well be much later than the upper part of the Durness Limestone but the youngest rocks they cut are believed to be of Cambrian age.

REFERENCES

1882. HEDDLE, M. F. On the Geognosy and Mineralogy of Scotland. *Mineralogical Mag.* vol. iv, p. 233.
1884. HEDDLE, M. F. *Mineralogical Mag.*, vol. v, p. 133.
1886. TEALL, J. J. H. Notes on some Hornblende-bearing Rocks from Inchnadamff. *Geol. Mag.*, dec. 3, vol. iii, p. 346.
1892. HORNE, J., and J. J. H. TEALL. On Borolanite; an Igneous Rock intrusive in the Cambrian of Assynt. *Trans. Roy. Soc. Edin.*, vol. xxxvii, pt. i, p. 163.
1900. TEALL, J. J. H. On Nepheline-Syenite and its Associates in the North-West of Scotland. *Geol. Mag.*, dec. 4, vol. vii, p. 386.
1906. SHAND, S. J. Ueber Borolanit und die Gesteine des Cnoc-na-Sroine Massivs in Nord Schottland. *Neues Jahrb.*, B.B. xxii, p. 413.

1907. TEALL, J. J. H. *In* The Geological Structure of the North-West Highlands of Scotland. *Mem. Geol. Surv.*, chaps xxx and xxxi.

1909, 1910. SHAND, S. J. On Borolanite and its Associates in Assynt. *Trans. Edin. Geol. Soc.*, vol. ix, pt. iii, p. 202, and pt. v, p. 376.

1926. PHEMISTER, J. *In* The Geology of Strath Oykell and Lower Loch Shin. *Mem. Geol. Surv.*, chap. iii.

1931. PHEMISTER, J. On a Carbonate-Rock at Bad na h'Achlaise, Assynt, Sutherland. *Sum. Prog. Geol. Surv.* for 1930, pt. iii, p. 58.

1934. BAILEY, E. B., and W. J. MCCALLIEN. Pre-Cambrian Association. B. Second Excursion, Scotland. *Geol. Mag.*, vol. lxxi, p. 549.

1941. STEWART, F. H. On Sulphatic Cancrinite and Anaclime (Eudnophite) from Loch Borolan, Assynt. *Mineralogical Mag.*, vol. xxvi, p. 1.

1952. SABINE, P. A. The Ledmorite dike of Achmelvich, near Lochinver, Sutherland. *Mineralogical Mag.*, vol. xxix, p. 827.

1953. SABINE, P. A. The petrography and geological significance of the Post-Cambrian Minor Intrusions of Assynt and the adjoining districts of North-West Scotland. *Quart. Journ. Geol. Soc.*, vol. cix, p. 137.

1958. TILLEY, C. E. Some new Chemical Data on Assemblages of the Assynt Alkali Suite. *Trans. Edin. Geol. Soc.*, vol. xvii, p. 156.

VII. POST-CAMBRIAN THRUST-MOVEMENTS

PASSING reference has been made in previous pages to the great thrust-movements which affected the Moine Schists and the Durness Limestone and older rocks of North-west Scotland. The zone of thrusts extends from Sleat in Skye to Whitten Head, a distance of 120 miles (Plate VII). Its width varies greatly. In Skye it is 12 miles wide, in Northern Ross-shire it is in places represented by a single thrust-plane, which separates Moine Schists from Cambrian sediments. Along its course in Sutherland the zone varies generally between 1 and 3 miles in width but in Assynt expands to 7 miles. In this area, while the base of the zone keeps its normal N.N.E. trend, the outcrop of the highest thrust— the Moine Thrust-plane—makes a wide semicircular sweep to the east owing to the denudation of a contemporaneous complex anticlinal fold (*see* p. 24). The section of the thrust-zone revealed by this combination of circumstances provides so many easily accessible examples of the anomalous stratigraphical results and of the rock-deformation produced by thrust-movement that the district has become classic ground for the study of this type of crustal fracture. Modifications of the original Geological Survey mapping and interpretation of the Glencoul and Ben More thrust-planes in the Assynt area have been made by E. B. Bailey (1935) and P. A. Sabine (1953).

Effects of the Thrust-movements.   The main fracture is the Moine Thrust. This dislocation dips generally at low angles to the E.S.E., and is usually well defined, but in places is represented by a narrow zone composed of mylonized schists and Cambrian strata without a definite plane of fracture. Above the Moine Thrust-plane lie the Moine Schists, beneath it is a zone of intensely disturbed Cambrian, Torridonian, and Lewisian rocks which are divided by great, but inconstant, thrust-planes into immense lenses, or nappes, each of which has been displaced west-north-westwards relatively to the underlying rocks. Within the thrust-zone Lewisian Gneiss may be superposed on Torridon Sandstone or on Cambrian strata (Plate I); Torridonian may rest on Cambrian (Plate IVb). Such inversions of the natural order are generally due to superposition of the more ancient rock on the younger by thrust-movement, but are sometimes due to isoclinal folds which vary in magnitude from small folds, produced by rolling motion along the thrust-plane, to great inversions affecting a large portion of a nappe. The major thrust-planes which carry the nappes are generally inclined at low angles but may be locally steep or folded. Minor thrust-planes with steep hade are frequent and are specially common in the Cambrian strata beneath the major thrust and at the base of the thrust-zone. Closely packed small thrusts of this type constitute *imbricate* structure, and result in apparent increase in the thickness of the strata (Figs. 14 and 15). The lowest plane of movement, or rather the approximately plane envelope of innumerable intersecting surfaces of carriage forming the lowest level of the thrust-zone, is known as the 'sole' and separates the disturbed rocks of the thrust-zone from the unmoved, or apparently unmoved, Lewisian, Torridonian and Cambrian below.

It is widely agreed that, in the immediate vicinity of the thrusts, the metamorphic effects of the thrust-movements are mainly of retrograde character.

Quartz and feldspar are mechanically broken down and the dark minerals are converted to chlorite, epidote, and iron ore. The ultimate product of mechanical reduction of the harder rocks is mylonite, a platy material usually colour-banded but so finely divided that the parent rock is often indeterminable. Mylonite is especially developed at the Moine Thrust-plane where the rocks involved in the mylonite may include gneiss, granulite, and quartzite. Detailed structural studies that include the mylonite zone have been made recently by M. R. W. Johnson (1956, 1957). Christie and others (1954) state that there has been repeated movement and older mylonites have been remylonitized.

Opinions differ as to whether, for some miles east of the main thrust, the dislocation metamorphism affected Moine Schists at a low or high temperature, and as to the time relationships of folding, regional metamorphism, and thrusting. These problems are discussed in the Geological Survey Memoir on Central Sutherland (Sheets 108 and 109) by H. H. Read and in papers by J. E. Richey (1948), W. Q. Kennedy (1948a, 1949, 1955), E. B. Bailey (1950, 1955), and A. G. MacGregor (1952).

In sheared rocks west of the Moine Thrust (in the 'Zone of Complication'), deformation of small structures is well shown in the Cambrian Pipe-rock and the Torridonian conglomerates. The pipes become flattened and are bent over in the direction of movement, and finally are reduced to ribbons streaking the shear-planes. Pebbles in conglomerate are drawn out, flattened, and fractured.

Displacement and Origin. The minimum distance through which the Moine Schists have been displaced westwards relative to the formations beneath the Moine Thrust-plane is estimated at 10 miles. In places the schists are super-posed on undisturbed Cambrian and therefore it is certain that movement along the Moine Thrust-plane continued longer than on the other thrusts. It is believed that the movements were also initiated along this plane.

Such great fractures must have been caused by intense compression in a W.N.W.-E.S.E. direction. Usually the movement is envisaged as transportation of the Moine Schists from the south-south-east toward the west-north-west, but it is perhaps more probable that the western formations moved south-south-east and forced the schists to rise over them.

Age. It is clear that there are thrust-movements younger than sills and laccoliths intrusive into the Cambrian and adjacent Moines of Assynt. It has, however, been suggested that some of the sills may have been intruded during a pause in the movements and may thus be of inter-thrustal age (Bailey and McCallien 1934; MacGregor 1952; Sabine 1953).

The movements are older than certain lamprophyric sheets of the 'Newer Granite' intrusive suite which are found emplaced along thrust-planes (p. 61). Moreover, pebbles of rocks sheared by the movements are found in Middle Old Red Sandstone conglomerate. The thrusts are therefore of Caledonian age, and since the lamprophyres referred to above may be sheared by renewed movement, it is at least possible that the thrusts belong to a late stage of the Caledonian orogenic period.

REFERENCES
(*See also References on* p. 93)

1861. NICOL, J. On the structure of the North-western Highlands and the Relations of the Gneiss, Red Sandstone, and Quartzite of Sutherland. *Quart. Journ. Geol. Soc.*, vol. xvii, p. 85.
1883. CALLAWAY, C. The Age of the Newer Gneissic Rocks of the Northern Highlands. *Quart. Journ. Geol. Soc.*, vol. xxxix, p. 355.

1883. LAPWORTH, C. The Secret of the Highlands. *Geol. Mag.*, dec. 2, vol. x, pp. 120, 193, 337.
1884. GEIKIE, Sir A. The Crystalline Rocks of the Scottish Highlands. *Nature*, vol. xxxi, p. 29.
1884. PEACH, B. N., and J. HORNE. Report on the Geology of the North-West of Sutherland. *Nature*, vol. xxxi, p. 31.
1885. LAPWORTH, C. On the Stratigraphy and Metamorphism of the Rocks of the Durness-Eiriboll District. *Proc. Geol. Assoc.*, vol. viii, p. 438.
1885. LAPWORTH, C. On the Close of the Highland Controversy. *Geol. Mag.*, dec. 3, vol. ii, p. 97.
1888. GEIKIE, Sir A. Report on the Recent Work of the Geological Survey in the North-West Highlands of Scotland. *Quart. Journ. Geol. Soc.*, vol. xliv, p. 389.
1889. CADELL, H. M. Experimental Researches in Mountain Building. *Trans. Roy. Soc. Edin.*, vol. xxxv, p. 337.
1907. PEACH, B. N., and others. The Geological Structure of the North-West Highlands of Scotland. *Mem. Geol. Surv.*
1930. PEACH, B. N., and J. HORNE. *Chapters on the Geology of Scotland.* Oxford.
1934. BAILEY, E. B. The Glencoul Nappe and the Assynt Culmination. *Geol. Mag.*, vol. lxxii, p. 151.
1939. BAILEY, E. B. Caledonian Tectonics and Metamorphism in Skye. *Bull. Geol. Surv. Gt. Brit.*, No. 2, p. 46.
1953. SABINE, P. A. The petrography and geological significance of the Post-Cambrian Minor Intrusions of Assynt and the adjoining districts of North-West Scotland. *Quart. Journ. Geol. Soc.*, vol. cix, p. 137.
1954. BAILEY, E. B. Relations of Torridonian to Durness Limestone in the Broadford-Strollamus District of Skye. *Geol. Mag.*, vol. xci, p. 73.
1955. BAILEY, E. B. Moine Tectonics and Metamorphism in Skye. *Trans. Edin. Geol. Soc.*, vol. xvi, pt. ii, p. 93.
    See also Geological Survey Memoirs (p. 104) on Glenelg, Central Ross-shire, and Fannich Mountains.

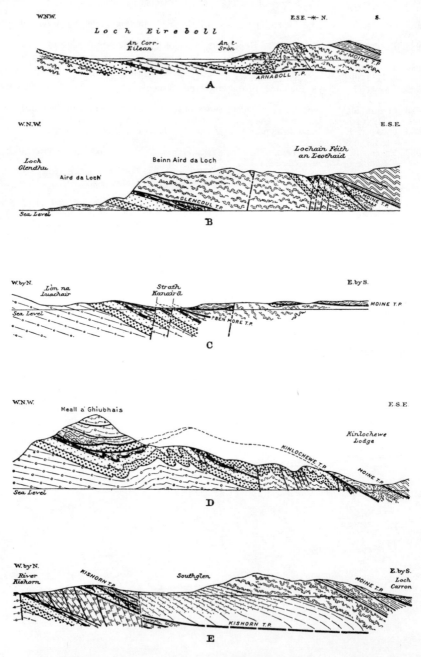

FIG. 14. *Sections across the post-Cambrian thrust-belt.*

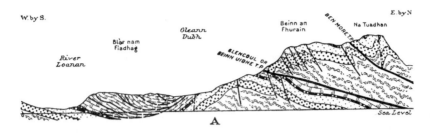

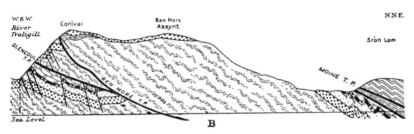

FIG. 15. *Sections across the post-Cambrian thrust-belt in Assynt.*

EXPLANATION
(Figs. 14 & 15)

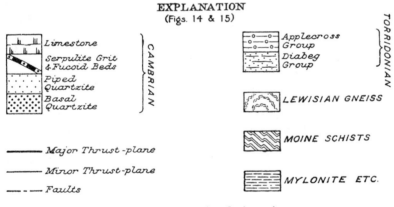

Fig. 14:—A. Section across Eireboll, a district of historical importance (1-inch Sheet 114). B. Illustrates a simple thrust-mass, or nappe; Lewisian Gneiss carried on a thrust-plane overlies Cambrian limestone (1-inch Sheet 107). C. Illustrates (i) faulting of a flat thrust-plane, and (ii) superposition of Moine Schists on unthrust Cambrian strata (1-inch Sheet 101). D. The section shows a klippe, or outlier of a nappe (1-inch Sheet 92). E. The section shows four major thrust-planes, two zones of imbricate structure, two zones of mylonite, and part of a reversed fold in which Lewisian Gneiss overlies Torridon Sandstone (1-inch Sheet 81).

Fig. 15:—The sections illustrate the structure of the thrust-belt in Assynt. Note: (i) the three major thrust-planes; (ii) overlap of the Glencoul by the Ben More Thrust-plane; (iii) the zone of imbrication above the 'sole'; (iv) the zone of mylonite above the Moine Thrust-plane; (v) superposition of Lewisian Gneiss and Torridon Sandstone above Cambrian strata. The west end of section B lies 1½ miles S.S.W. of the east end of Section A.

VIII.   NEWER IGNEOUS ROCKS

IGNEOUS rocks intruded after the regional and injection metamorphisms of the Moine Series are numerous in the Northern Highlands. They fall into two main divisions, the earlier including the intrusions of pre-Middle Old Red Sandstone age, the later comprising suites of minor intrusions of widely differing ages (p. 82). In this section the earlier division is described; the intrusions are varied both in composition and form and are for convenience subdivided as follows:

Syenites of Loch Loyal area	..	? LACCOLITH
Foliated lamprophyre	..	SHEETS AND DYKES
Ach'uaine Hybrid and Appinite Suites	..	MINOR INTRUSIONS
Granite, granodiorite, and diorite ..	..	STOCKS AND BATHOLITHS
Later hypabyssal intrusions	..	SHEETS AND DYKES

The distribution of these intrusions is shown in Figs. 16 and 17.

LOCH LOYAL SYENITES

The syenites around Loch Loyal have been studied recently by King, who separates them into three distinct masses which are intrusive into and contact-alter siliceous and semi-pelitic Moine Schists. He suggests that the largest, the Ben Loyal mass, and the smallest, the Cnoc nan Cuilean mass, have the form of irregular cones narrowing downwards, but the relations of the former to the country rock seem rather to be those of a sheet or laccolith fed from a flank, and the relations of the latter are those of a stock. The third mass, lying east of Loch Loyal, comprises sheets in part transgressive, in part concordant to the foliation of the Moine Schists. Several large inclusions of Moine granulite, up to 400 yds in length, lie within the Ben Loyal mass.

The main rock of the intrusions varies in composition from quartzose syenite with biotite and hornblende to alkali-syenite containing aegirine-augite. It shows neither foliation nor cataclasis. The powdery yellow mineral occurring in drusy cavities in the syenite has been reported recently as a new, hydrated species with the structure of monazite (Knorring and Dearnley 1959). The alkali-syenite is chemically and petrographically identical with the pulaskite of the Loch Ailsh laccolith, and in view of the rarity of this type of igneous rock in Scotland it is probable that the Ben Loyal and Loch Ailsh intrusions are coeval. This correlation, if correct, suggests interesting deductions; for example, that the Ben Loyal syenite, though not sheared, is earlier than the Moine Thrust; that since the Ben Loyal syenite contact-alters Moine schists, the latter were crystalline before the Moine Thrust-plane developed (*see also* p. 36).

In the Cnoc nan Cuilean intrusion basic syenites of variable composition occupy the marginal zone and dykes of similar character appear in the granulites exposed in the Allt Torr an Tairbh. The dykes are described by King as grading into basic granulites carrying aegirine-augite and hornblende produced by metasomatic reactions.

Veins of syenite cut the surrounding schists and veins of pegmatitic syenite cut the main intrusion. An erratic block of this pegmatite contained the rare mineral thorite.

FOLIATED LAMPROPHYRES

Foliated lamprophyres have been found from central Ross-shire southwards to the Ross of Mull. They are present also in the Grampian Highlands and were studied by W. B. Wright in Colonsay. They occur both as dykes and sheets which may follow or transgress the foliation of the schists. In Morvern (Argyllshire) they follow joints. Generally quite thin, they range up to 15 ft in thickness. Some are completely foliated; others show foliation only at the margins. The direction of foliation is parallel to the walls and may make any angle with the direction of foliation in the schists. Contact-alteration of the latter has occasionally been observed.

The less sheared members are recognizable as biotite-vogesites and minettes of the same type as the later lamprophyres (p. 67), from which they are distinguished by evidence of cataclasis, recrystallization of quartz and feldspar, and production of green biotite, epidote, and sphene. The more completely foliated types, the lampro-schists, are green lustrous rocks with twisted foliation in which all igneous texture has been destroyed; petrographically they are calcareous hornblende-biotite-schists. The massive unfoliated centres of the larger intrusions cannot be distinguished from the unfoliated lamprophyres.

ACH'UAINE HYBRID AND APPINITE SUITE

This group of minor intrusions exhibits a great variety of rock-types, which vary in composition from ultrabasic to acid. Small masses may be entirely of ultrabasic or intermediate composition but commonly the intrusions show great diversity of composition. The group includes the appinites of Argyllshire and the rocks described in Sutherland as Hybrids of Ach'uaine Type. Intrusions with similar petrological characters are widely scattered through the Grampian Highlands. In the Northern Highlands the intrusions have the form of small bosses, sills and dykes, and tend to occur in groups, but isolated members remote from the groups are also known. They appear to be absent from central and southern Ross-shire, and it is probably of significance that this area contains no 'Newer Granite' stocks.

Ultrabasic. The best known of the ultrabasic members is scyelite, a biotite-hornblende-peridotite. In some specimens biotite is rare and the rock is a cortlandtite. Hornblende-pyroxene-rocks are often associated with scyelite and also form independent intrusions. The rocks are not foliated, the only alteration being of a juvenile character and resulting in conversion of olivine and pyroxene to serpentine, tremolite, chlorite, magnetite, and talc. In the north of the region all the varieties are widespread, but in the Loch Linnhe region hornblende-pyroxene-rock is the commonest type.

Basic to Acid members often occur together, the same exposure showing syenitic or granitic, basic, and sometimes ultrabasic rock, but homogeneous intrusions are also known. Alkali-feldspar and quartz persist in the basic varieties, and perthitic feldspar and oligoclase occur in all relative proportions. The dark minerals are hornblende, biotite—often poikilitic—and pyroxene. Sphene and apatite are often very abundant. Petrographically, therefore, the rocks include granite, monzonite and diorite, and the mesocratic varieties may be syenitic or dioritic. Though the intrusions are small the grain is usually coarse. The sheets and dykes of appinite in Morvern average 15 ft and reach

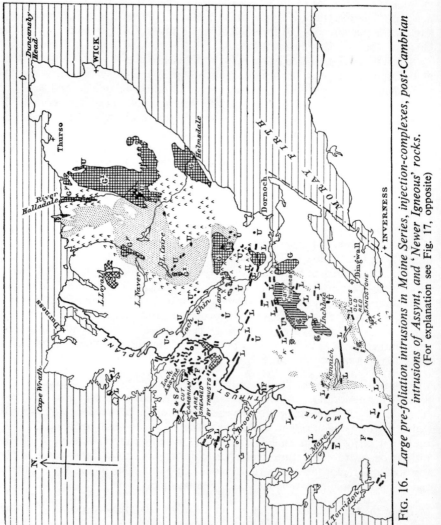

Fig. 16. *Large pre-foliation intrusions in Moine Series, injection-complexes, post-Cambrian intrusions of Assynt, and 'Newer Igneous' rocks.* (For explanation see Fig. 17, opposite)

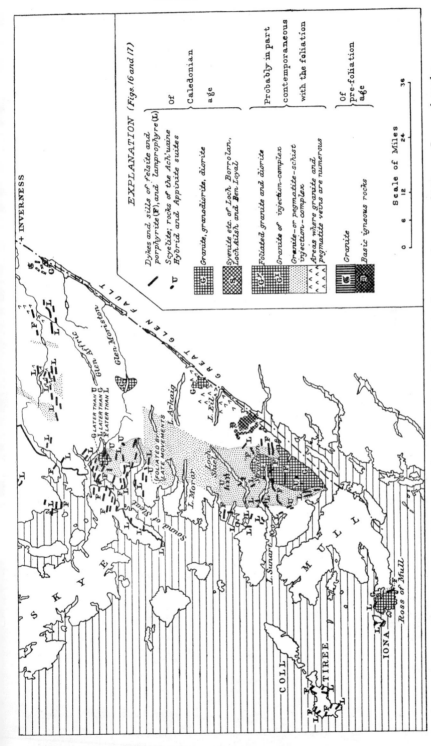

Fig. 17. *Large pre-foliation intrusions in Moine Series, injection-complexes, and 'Newer Igneous' rocks.*

30 ft in thickness, while the average dimensions of the bosses of Ach'uaine Hybrid type are 200 by 50 yds.

The variable composition is a regional property of the suite, and was regarded by Read as due to hybridism between ultrabasic rock and the granite of the regional injection-complexes. Typical intrusions of the suite, however, occur in Sutherland remote from the regional injection-complexes, and the latter are in Argyllshire cut by sheets of appinite. Yet at Knockfinn in Sutherland biotite-pyroxene-hornblendite, regarded by Read as allied to the Ach'uaine Hybrids, is cut by veins of red granite presumably connected with the Strath Halladale Granite, within the outcrop of which the ultrabasic rock lies. Again, within the Loch Coire complex ultrabasic and basic rocks of Ach'uaine Hybrid type are associated with granite of a type which forms masses and veins within the injection-gneisses. The writer has already advanced the view (p. 34) that the injection-granites are of early Caledonian age, and the conflicting evidence outlined above may be reconciled by supposing that the later phases of the injection-period overlapped the period of intrusion of the Ach'uaine Hybrid rocks.

The group under description has more definite associations with the 'Newer Granite' stocks. Within the latter ultrabasic and basic masses of Ach'uaine Hybrid or Appinite type are commonly enclosed, as, for example, in the Ben Ratagain, Strontian, and Lairg Granites. Similar association with the Newer Granites is found in the Grampian Highlands, and these ultrabasic and basic rocks are generally regarded as early phases of the intrusive period of the granites.

The facts of regional distribution and persistent variability in mineral composition suggest the simultaneous existence of ultrabasic and quartzo-feldspathic magmas below large stretches of the crust and indicate some spatial connection between these magmas so that intrusion of ultrabasic was in many cases followed soon by intrusion of acidic magma along the same channel. The existence of more homogenous bodies of appinite and ultrabasic rock suggests that in places migration had occurred.

The minor intrusions described above are in general unfoliated, but some appinites show flow-structure. A member of the Ach'uaine Hybrid suite near the Moine Thrust-plane in Sutherland is foliated, and south of Loch Hourn also a large dyke which appears to belong to this group is foliated.

GRANITE—GRANODIORITE—DIORITE

The table shows the various stocks and batholiths of 'Newer Granite' which occur in the Northern Highlands, the arrangement being from north to south downwards.

NAME OF INTRUSION	OUTCROP	ROCK-TYPES
Reay	2½ sq. miles	Augite-biotite-diorite, augite-granite.
Helmsdale	38 ,,	Adamellite, porphyritic and non-porphyritic.
Lairg	27 ,,	Granodiorite and biotite-granite.
Grudie	1 ,,	Adamellite with much quartz.
Migdale	9 ,,	Adamellite.
Fearn	12 ,,	Adamellite.
Ràtagain	5 ,,	Granite, diorite, syenite, adamellite.
Cluanie	7 ,,	Granodiorite.
Glen Loy	5¾ ,,	Diorite, appinite, hornblendite, potassic microcline-granite.
Strontian	80 ,,	Tonalite, granodiorite, biotite-granite.
Ross of Mull	20 ,,	Hornblende-biotite-diorite, muscovite-biotite-granite

In many of these masses multiple intrusion has occurred, the most basic rock having been emplaced first, the most acid last, but, in general, intrusion of the later components has followed so quickly that chilled contacts are unusual. Reference has already been made (p. 64) to the presence of early very basic or ultrabasic masses in the Lairg, Ratagain, and Strontian Granites. Flow-structure is apparent in the tonalitic or dioritic components of the Lairg, Ratagain, Strontian, and Ross of Mull masses, but is non-existent in the more acid granodiorites and the granites. Concentric disposition of the components is found at Helmsdale and at Strontian (Fig. 18); in both cases the outer component is the earlier.

Relationships between major and trace elements in the tonalite, granodiorite, and granite of the Strontian Complex have been studied by S. R. Nockolds and L. R. Mitchell (1948) and compared with those of other Caledonian plutonic complexes south of the Great Glen (Garabal, Ben Nevis, Arrochar, Moy, Carn Chois, &c.)

It should be noted that though the Reay Granite is included here among the Newer Granites, little is known about this intrusion, except that it is not granulitized, it is fluxional rather than foliated, and contains bronzy biotites resembling those of the scyelites.

Detailed information regarding the contact-relations of the Newer Granites is in many cases lacking, but sufficient is known to demonstrate wide variation.

Relations to the Country-rock. The Helmsdale mass has vertical walls and exerts very slight contact-alteration in the adjacent siliceous schists. The boundary of the tonalite at Strontian, the outer component, is generally vertical but at parts dips inwards at angles of 70 to 45 degrees. The biotite-granite forms an intricate stockwork of sheets and dykes cutting the tonalite, granodiorite, and the schists on the east of the mass. No contact-alteration has been observed, but the strike of the schists is powerfully diverted at the north end so as to conform with the margin of the tonalite; the more resistant bands of the country-rock have been broken into masses round which the softer schists have flowed. Diversion of strike occurs also on the south and south-west margin of the Ràtagain intrusion, but may be due in whole or in part to wrench-faulting, and locally a breccia of schist cemented by granite borders the intrusion. The microcline-granite of Glen Loy, which is not well exposed, appears to form a sheeted complex which cuts across the more basic igneous rocks and extends into the adjacent schists.

A feature of many of the intrusions is the presence of a marginal zone of veins. Thus the Migdale and Fearn Granites inject a plexus of granite into the schists on their north and east margins. The western and southern contacts are sharp, and only slight contact-alteration of the schists is observed. The Ràtagain intrusion is fringed on its western margin by small masses and veins so that the boundary between the main intrusion and the schists is difficult to place. The intrusion is not chilled and the schists are not appreciably contact-altered, but chlorite in Lewisian Gneiss is altered to biotite.

The relations between granite and schist become much more intimate in the case of the Lairg and Ross of Mull Granites. Along the northern margin of the former there appears a zone in which granite and schist are intermixed. The zone increases in width eastwards and on the eastern margin widens to 3 miles. Nearest the granite the schists within the zone form layers of inclusions soaked with granitic material so that the edges are ill-defined. Outwards from the main granite the proportion of schist increases and the granitic material forms lit-par-lit intrusions along the foliation. Towards the outer edge of the zone the igneous part of the complex forms transgressive veins breaking up the schists into great xenoliths. This outer part thus resembles the vein-network bordering the Migdale and Fearn Granites. The granite of the marginal com-

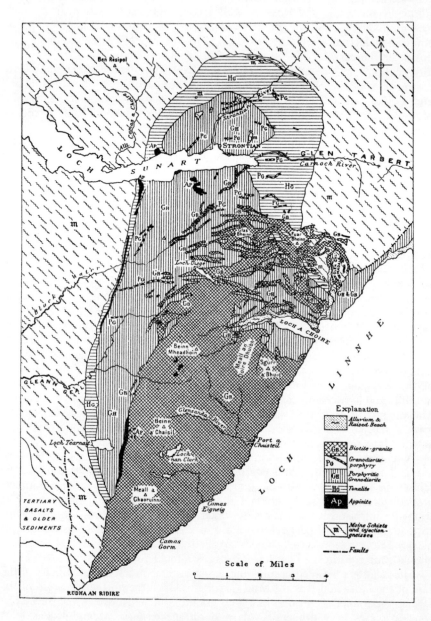

FIG. 18. *The Strontian Granite.*
(Partly taken from manuscript Geological Survey Map, one-inch Sheet 52.)

plex is biotite-granite, the schists are. mainly siliceous and have experienced only an increase in grain size.

Injection-phenomena at the margin of the Ross of Mull Granite are similar to those associated with the Lairg Granite, but xenoliths of schist, from fragments to immense masses, appear also in the southern and eastern part of the main intrusion. Every variation is found between sharp-edged·inclusion and 'ghosts' representing thoroughly permeated schists. The marginal injection-zone lies on the east side, but since on the west and south the intrusion is bounded by the sea, it is not known whether the injection-zone is limited to this side. The zone is a few hundred yards across and contains banded gneisses formed by lit-par-lit injection of granitic material into the siliceous granulites and coarse gneisses formed by less regular injection and permeation of the mica-schists. The Ross of Mull and Glen Loy intrusions appear to be the only Newer Granites of the Northern Highlands which have produced intense contact-alteration. In the Ross of Mull, where cordierite, andalusite, and sillimanite have been formed, W. S. Mackenzie (1949) has found that large regional kyanite crystals have been altered to andalusite. In Glen Loy, contact-altered schists close to dioritic rocks locally contain cordierite, while sillimanite in crystals up to 3 in. long is abundant.

The injection-zones and zones of veins have been described, in the case of the Lairg, Fearn, and Ross of Mull Granites, as occurring in the roof. It is noteworthy that these zones, when present, occur on the north and east margins of the intrusions except in the single case of the Ràtagain Granite.

It is of interest to note that muscovite-pegmatites associated with the Fearn Granite contain garnet and tourmaline where they cut the schists.

LATER HYPABYSSAL INTRUSIONS

Dykes and sills of felsite and porphyrite are in general restricted to the vicinity of certain of the Newer Granites. The more acid intrusions average about 15 ft and reach 60 ft in thickness, while the more basic porphyrites average about 10 feet and may attain a thickness of 20 feet. The dykes are often continuous for 2 or 3 miles, and in Morvern a felsite dyke has been traced interruptedly for 7 miles and a porphyrite for 12 miles. In the Glenelg district and in Sleat the trend of the dykes associated with the Ràtagain Granite varies from E.-W. to E.N.E.-W.S.W. In Iona and the Ross of Mull the felsites and porphyrites occur mainly as sheets. Within and around the Strontian Granite the dykes of this group trend generally E.-W. Petrographically the felsites and porphyrites are of the usual Lower Old Red Sandstone type—that is, they vary from felsite through quartz-albite-porphyrite and biotite-porphyrite to hornblende-porphyrite which grades into spessartite.

Many of the thicker sheets in Iona are composite, the central portion consisting of acid porphyrite while the marginal rock is micro-diorite or lamprophyre. The porphyrite was emplaced after intrusion of the more basic portion of the sheet, though possibly in some cases the earlier part was not quite consolidated before the intrusion of the more acid rock.

The lamprophyres include minette, kersantite, vogesite, and spessartite and present no primary distinctions from the foliated lamprophyres. They are generally thinner than the porphyrites and seldom attain a thickness of more than 10 ft, the thickest members being those minettes which are not definitely associated with any particular granitic intrusion. The hornblendic types, vogesite and spessartite, are found mainly in the neighbourhood of the granites, while the biotite-lamprophyres are more widely distributed and show less tendency to occur in local swarms. In Iona and the Ross of Mull the lampro-phyres appear to occur mainly as sills or sheets with moderate inclination, but elsewhere they form dykes which trend in general E.-W. but vary in direction between N.W.-S.E. and W.S.W.-E.N.E. The hornblendic types are panidio-morphic rocks, which show varieties transitional to appinite. Transition between spessartite and microdiorite is found and yields types comparable with the luciites and orbites of the Odenwald. The mica-lamprophyres are mainly augite-minettes and, though kersantites are not common, the minettes usually contain some acid plagioclase. Pseudomorphs after olivine are sometimes present, and apatite is always very abundant. Xenoliths are of frequent occur-rence in the minettes and sometimes are very numerous. They may include a quite large proportion of rocks not found in the immediate country-rock. For example, a minette cutting Moine granulites in south-west Sutherland contains, in addition to xenocrysts of quartz and xenoliths of granulite, many enclaves of Lewisian gneiss and some of lamproschist.

Outer Hebrides. Intrusions which possibly belong to the Caledonian igneous period are poorly represented in the Outer Hebrides. Jehu and Craig refer to a few spessartites in South Harris and North Uist and to a single augite-kersantite in South Uist.

AGE RELATIONS

Conglomerate of Middle Old Red Sandstone age is cut by minette near Loch Garve, Ross-shire, while pebbles of the same igneous type are found in the Middle Old Red Sandstone conglomerates of Meall a' Ghrianain, Ross-shire. The mica-lamprophyres therefore have a wide range in time. Felsite, porphyrite, and lamprophyres all cut the granites and are therefore younger. Though these minor intrusions are all of the same general age, evidence of the relative order of their emplacement has occasionally been obtained. Thus, lamprophyre and porphyrite both cut felsite, while both hornblende- and mica-lamprophyres are known to be earlier, though in some cases only slightly earlier, than porphyrite.

Determination of the precise age of the granites is a matter of difficulty. The Helmsdale and Fearn Granites are earlier than the local Middle Old Red Sandstone; the Ross of Mull Granite, or an apophysis of it, is believed to cross the Moine Thrust-plane between Iona and the Ross of Mull; the Strontian and Ràtagain Granites are younger than unfoliated basic and ultrabasic rocks. The granites show neither foliation not cataclasis, except of local crush origin. In their composite structure and detailed petrography they resemble the Newer Granite stocks and batholiths of the Central Highlands and Southern Uplands, all of which are later than the Caledonian folding while many are of later date than sediments of Lower Old Red Sandstone age. There is therefore good reason to regard the granites as intruded during Lower Old Red Sandstone or possibly late Silurian times.

The minor intrusions of variable composition, including scyelite and the Appinite and Ach'uaine Hybrid Suites, are in all cases where definite evidence is available earlier than the granite stocks and batholiths. They are, however, regarded on mineralogical grounds as cognate with the granites and therefore of the same general age. Some appinites show flow-structure, and occasionally members of this group are foliated. The period of intrusion, therefore, probably began before that of the thrust-movement was finally closed. The foliated lamprophyres are apparently an older group, since they have been found xenolithic in appinite and in the later lamprophyres. Since they are intrusive along thrust-planes they are later than the thrust-movements. It is probable that their foliation is indicative of high susceptibility to change under slight shearing stress rather than proof of another period of powerful stress subsequent to the thrust-movements.

The age of the Ben Loyal Syenite relative to the other Newer Igneous Rocks is not known with certainty. G. D. Nicholls (1951) has thrown doubt on the inference that the Ben Loyal and Loch Ailsh syenites are coeval. If however these intrusions are contemporaneous, the Ben Loyal syenite must be older than the thrust-movements and consequently considerably earlier than even the foliated lamprophyric and basic members of the Newer Igneous Rocks. The precise position of the Assynt laccolites and minor intrusions in the long time-interval between late Cambrian times and the period of thrust-movement has not been established. Reference has already been made to the fact that certain alkaline sills (allied to the Assynt porphyrites) were intruded into Moine granulites close to the Moine Thrust and have been affected by the thrust-movements (p. 56). It may be noted that petrographic similarity is strong between the Assynt felsites and porphyrites and those of Lower Old Red Sandstone age, and that considerable chemical similarity exists between the vogesite sills of Assynt, the shonkinite of Loch Ailsh, certain of the Ach'uaine Hybrids and one of the kentallenites of Argyllshire. Moreover, alkali-syenite occurs as a minor component of the Ràtagain mass, of the appinite suite in Moidart, and of a kentallenite intrusion at Glen Coe.

The Reay Diorite is older than the local Middle Old Red Sandstone, but whether it is contemporaneous with the regional injecting granites or a member of the Newer Igneous Rocks is not known.

REFERENCES

1878. GEIKIE, Sir A. On the Old Red Sandstone of Western Europe. *Trans. Roy. Soc. Edin.*, vol. xxviii, p. 406.
1884. HEDDLE, M. F. Geognosy and Mineralogy of Scotland—Sutherland—part iv. *Mineralogical Mag.*, vol. v, p. 133.
1885. JUDD, J. W. On the Tertiary and Older Peridotites of Scotland. *Quart. Journ. Geol. Soc.*, vol. xli, p. 401.
1897-99. GRANT WILSON, J. S. In *Sum. Prog. Geol. Surv.* for 1897, p. 65; for 1898, p. 42; for 1899, p. 39.
1911. BOSWORTH, T. O. Metamorphism around the Ross of Mull Granite. *Quart. Journ. Geol. Soc.*, vol. lxvi, p. 376.
1918. HARKER, A. Presidential Address. *Quart. Journ. Geol. Soc.*, vol. lxxiii, p. lxxxvi.
1922. JEHU, T. J. The Archaean and Torridonian Formations and the Later Intrusive Igneous Rocks of Iona. *Trans. Roy. Soc. Edin.*, vol. liii, p. 178.
1928. SCOTT, J. F. General Geology and Physiography of Morvern. *Trans. Geol. Soc. Glasgow*, vol. xviii, pt. i, p. 149.
1932. MACGREGOR, A. G., and W. Q. KENNEDY. The Morvern-Strontian Granite. *Sum. Prog. Geol. Surv.* for 1931, pt. ii, p. 105.
1939. RICHEY, J. E. The Dykes of Scotland. *Trans. Edin. Geol. Soc.*, vol. xiii, pt. iv, p. 393.
1943. KING, B. C. The Cnoc nan Cuilean Area of the Ben Loyal Igneous Complex. *Quart. Journ. Geol. Soc.*, vol. xcviii, p. 147.
1948. NOCKOLDS, S. R., and R. L. MITCHELL. The Geochemistry of some Caledonian Plutonic Rocks: a Study in the Relationship between the Major and Trace Elements of Igneous Rocks and their Minerals. *Trans. Roy. Soc. Edin.*, vol. lxi, pt. ii, p. 533.
1949. MACKENZIE, W. S. Kyanite-Gneiss within a Thermal Aureole. *Geol. Mag.*, vol. lxxxvi, p. 251.

1951. NICHOLLS, G. D.   The Glenelg-Ratagain Igneous Complex. *Quart. Journ. Geol. Soc.*, vol. cvi, p. 309.

1951. NICHOLLS, G. D.   An Unusual Pyroxene-rich Zenolith in the Diorite of the Glenelg-Ratagain Igneous Complex. *Geol. Mag.*, vol. lxxxviii, p. 284.

1952. LEEDAL, G. P.   The Cluanie igneous intrusion, Inverness-shire and Ross-shire. *Quart. Journ. Geol. Soc.*, vol. cviii, p. 35.

1953-59. MACGREGOR, A. G., and others.   In *Sum. Prog. Geol. Surv.*, for 1951, p. 44; for 1952, p. 36; for 1953, p. 48; for 1954, p. 48; for 1958, p. 43.

1959. KNORRING, O. von, and R. DEARNLEY.   A note on a nordmarkite and an associated rare-earth mineral from the Ben Loyal syenite complex, Sutherlandshire. *Notice No. 107, Mineralogical Soc.*

See also Geological Survey Memoirs (p. 104) on Iona, Ben Nevis, Glenelg, Central Ross-shire, Beauly, Lower Findhorn, Fannich Mountains, Ben Wyvis, Strath Oykell, Golspie, Central Sutherland, and Caithness.

IX. OLD RED SANDSTONE

NORTH of the Grampians the Old Red Sandstone is separated into two divisions the higher of which, the Upper Old Red Sandstone, rests unconformably on the lower division. The latter constitutes the Middle Old Red Sandstone of Scotland and is known also as the Orcadian Series. It yields a rich fossil fauna consisting mainly of fishes which are allied to those of the Upper Old Red, and so are markedly distinct from the fishes of the Lower Old Red strata south of the Grampians which have closer affinity with the Silurian. Moreover, the flora of the Middle Old Red Sandstone of the North is quite different from that of the Lower division in Central Scotland.

In the Northern Highlands Old Red Sandstone strata form an almost continuous outcrop from Loch Ness to the north coast of Caithness. They form the western coast of the Moray Firth except where inliers of older rocks (schist and granite) protrude or where large N.N.E. faults have let down Mesozoic strata. West of the main outcrop many outliers indicate the former wide extension of the formation over the schists (Figs. 19 and 21). In the south of the region sediments which are probably of Middle Old Red Sandstone age appear only in small outliers of conglomerate caught between two branches of the Great Glen Fault at Rudha na h' Earba on the west shore of Loch Linnhe.

In a recent paper McIntyre and others (1956) have queried the Middle Old Red Sandstone age of conglomerate outliers near Tongue in Sutherland; the presence of boulders of Cambrian rocks and Ben Loyal syenite was not confirmed and therefore they suggest that Nicol's early correlation of these conglomerates with the Torridonian has not been disproved.

MIDDLE OLD RED SANDSTONE

CAITHNESS

The strata have been divided into lithological groups, some of which contain characteristic fossils, and have been correlated with the groups distinguished in the Orkneys, as shown in the table below:

LITHOLOGICAL GROUPS		CHARACTERISTIC FOSSIL	ORKNEY EQUIVALENT
John o' Groat's Sandstone ..		*Tristichopterus alatus*	Eday Sandstone
Caithness Flagstone Series	Thurso Flagstone Group	*Coccosteus minor*	Rousay Flags Stromness Beds
	Achanarras Band ..	Cromarty Firth fauna (pp. 67-68)	Sandwick Fish Bed
	Passage Group ..		Stromness Beds
	Wick Flagstone Group	No characteristic forms ..	—
Barren Red Series		—	—

The **Barren Red Series** consists of a lower group of arkose, conglomerate, and mudstone and an upper group of breccia, arkose, sandstone, and flagstone which unconformably overlies, and in places overlaps, the lower. The prevailing colours of the strata are red and chocolate, but green bands are common in the mudstones and flags. Where the higher members overlap on to the schist floor

71

fringing breccias of local rock form the basal deposits (Fig. 20). The overlap is in part due to the presence of ancient north-south ridges in the floor, but the series also diminishes in thickness northwards and at Blar Cnoc na Gaoith fossiliferous beds of the Caithness Flagstone Series rest directly on schist and granite. In the south of Caithness the thickness of the Series is estimated to vary from 1,600 to 3,000 ft.

Similar strata form outliers near Tongue and in Central Sutherland. The outlier which builds the islands Eilean nan Ron and Eilean Iosail at the entrance to the Kyle of Tongue is of importance on account of the presence of mylonitized rock in the conglomerate.

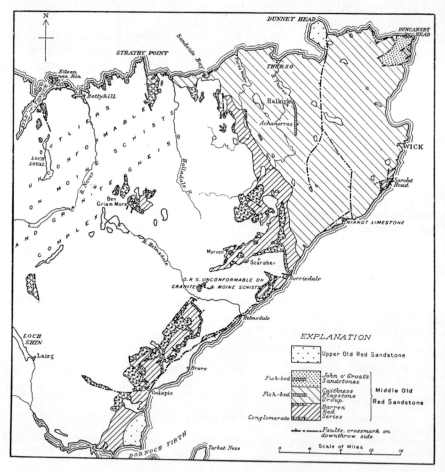

FIG. 19. *The Old Red Sandstone of Caithness and Sutherland.*

Caithness Flagstone Series. The lowest group, the Wick Flagstones, shows an abrupt change from the red strata of the Barren Red Series to pale sandstone, greenish-white mudstone, dark or black bituminous flags, and thin limestones. Fishes are obtained from the limestone bands of this group and are mainly *Thursius macrolepidotus* and *Dipterus valenciennesi*. The Passage Beds,

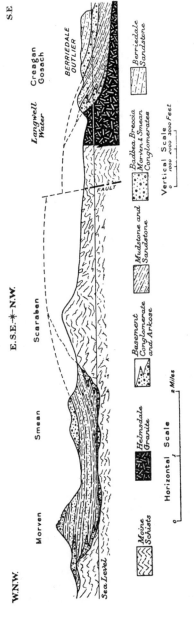

FIG. 20. *Section from Morven to Berriedale, illustrating unconformity of basal Middle Old Red Sandstone on Moine Schists and 'Newer' granite, the occurrence of fringing breccias, and intraformational unconformity.*

consisting of pale mudstones and calcareous flags with some comparatively thick and pure limestones, are bounded at the top by the 'Achanarras Band', a hard limy flagstone which has yielded an abundant and characteristic fish-fauna. The fish include *Diplacanthus striatus, Rhadinacanthus longispinus, Cheiracanthus murchisoni, Pterichthys milleri, P. productus, P. oblongus, Dipterus valenciennesi, Coccosteus decipiens, Homosteus milleri, Glyptolepis paucidens, Gyroptychius [Diplopterus] agassizi, Osteolepis macrolepidotus, Cheirolepis trailli.* This fauna is identical with that of the fish-beds of Cromarty (p. 75) and of the Stromness Beds in Orkney. The small lamprey-like creature *Palaeospondylus gunni* has been obtained only from this horizon in Caithness. In the Thurso Flagstone group flagstones are again dominant. Generally they are pale ochre or bluish in colour and only locally possess the dark appearance of those of the Wick group. The Thurso Flagstones have yielded a rich fauna including *Homacanthus borealis, Rhadinacanthus longispinus, Mesacanthus peachi, Cheiracanthus sp., Coccosteus decipiens, C. minor, Homosteus milleri, Dipterus valenciennesi, Glyptolepis paucidens, Thursius macrolepidotus, T. pholidotus, Osteolepis panderi, Gyroptychius milleri.* The fish fauna of Achanarras has been studied by C. Forster-Cooper (1937); he infers that *Dipterus valenciennesi* and *D. platycephalus* are two forms of one species and that *D. platycephalus* becomes a synonym for *D. valenciennesi.* The structure of *Rhamphodapsis* has been described by D. M. S. Watson (1938); T. S. Westoll (1936) and Jarvik (1948) have made a further study of *Osteolepis.*

A characteristic feature of the Series is the persistent repetition of sequences of sandstone, mudstone, calcareous flags, and limestone. This recurrence of cycles of sedimentation, the abundance of ripple-marks, sun-cracks and current-bedding, the absence of marine fossils and presence of land plants prove the landlocked character of the basin in which the strata were deposited. The limestones are chemical deposits. There is no evidence that the sea ever had access to this basin; on the contrary, the facts that many of the fossil fish are confined to the Orcadian region and that *Estheria*, a fresh or brackish water arthropod, is abundant in some beds, emphasize the lack of connection with the open sea. To the basin in which the Orcadian facies of the Old Red Sandstone accumulated, Sir A. Geikie gave the name Lake Orcadie. The total thickness of the Caithness Flagstone Series has been estimated at 14,500 ft.

The famous paving stones of Caithness are obtained from the flagstone groups, the first quality flags being provided by the most calcareous seams in the Thurso group. Very thin-splitting flags have been quarried as stoneslates.

The **John o' Groat's Sandstones** show an abrupt lithological change from the underlying series. They introduce the Upper Old Red Sandstone type of sedimentation and consist of yellow and red calcareous friable sandstones which are very false-bedded and contain small clay-galls. The thickness is at least 2,000 ft and there is possibly an unconformity at the base. Fossil fish are found in a few thin bands of pale weathering flagstone. They include *Microbrachius dicki, Dipterus macropterus, Tristichopterus alatus, Mesacanthus peachi,* and *Glyptolepis leptopterus,* and are in the main peculiar to this division of the Middle Old Red Sandstone.

In the Strathie outlier on the north coast fish-remains, including *Dipterus macropterus,* have been obtained a short distance above the local base. Since this species appears to be characteristic of the John o' Groat's Sandstones, very strong overlap is indicated.

CROMARTY FIRTH AREA

The Middle Old Red Sandstone strata are disposed in a great syncline, complicated by anticlinal folding and faults (Fig. 21). The basement conglomerates, breccias, and mudstones are therefore exposed along the western margin, in the district south-west of Inverness and on the east side of the Black Isle. On the eastern flank of the syncline the floor of metamorphic rocks reaches the surface at Rosemarkie and the Sutors of Cromarty.

The strata show the same general lithological succession as in Caithness, but are not developed in such force. Overlap of higher members on to the schist floor has been observed. The series differs from the Caithness succession lithologically in the absence of dark flagstones and palaeontologically in the occurrence of only the Achanarras type of fauna. Lateral variation is pronounced, as is shown in the following table of local successions and in the section (Fig. 22):

ALNESS	STRATHPEFFER TO DINGWALL	CROMARTY	BLACK ISLE (SOUTH-EAST HALF)
Yellow sandstones, green and red shales, grey shales with *Psilophyton* and nodular limestone containing ichthyolites at Edderton	Red and yellow sandstones, marly clays and shales	Red and yellow sandstones with Cromarty and Ethie Fish Beds	Millbuie Sandstone, Series (2,500 ft.) containing bluish calcareous shale with plants and bituminous beds with limestone nodules containing fish (Killen Burn Fish Bed)
Red and yellow sandstones with pebbly bands, passing down into conglomerate	Variable conglomerate passing up and down into red sandstones and shales	Basal conglomerate	Conglomerate and sandstone series (7,000 ft.). Two groups of conglomerate are separated by red sandstones and shales. The conglomerates thin out to the north-east and in this direction a band of shale with limestone nodules occurs in the sandstone-shale group.
Green and grey shales, flagstones, fetid dark shales and calcareous mudstones	Olive shales and fetid calcareous and bituminous shales with thin limestones (1,300 ft.)		
Basal breccia and conglomerate	Red and yellow sandstone and conglomerate		

Certain items of general interest may be noted. The conglomerates of the second highest group in the Alness district contain pebbles of Cambrian and Torridonian rocks but none of the augen-gneiss of Inchbae. It is possible that the absence of the latter indicates the extension of earlier Old Red Sandstone strata over the augen-gneiss region.

In the fetid shaly group of Strathpeffer the sulphurous springs which have made this village famous as a spa have their origin. The extension southward of this group is indicated by the occurrence of a sulphurous well at Beauly.

The highest group of the series contains the well-known Edderton, Cromarty, Ethie, and Killen Burn fish-beds which were first described by Hugh Miller.

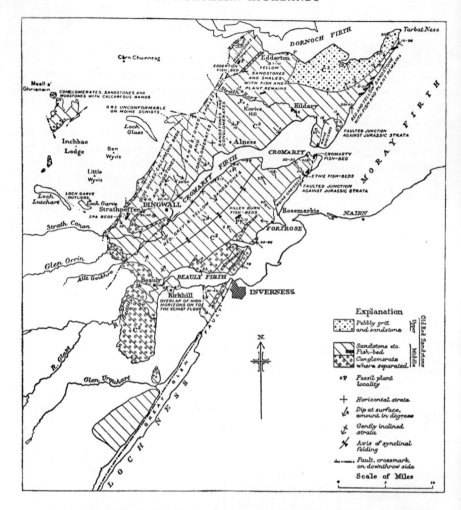

FIG. 21. *The Old Red Sandstone of Ross-shire and part of Inverness-shire.*

The fauna is closely comparable with the Achanarras fauna of Caithness and is the same as that obtained from the fish-beds of Moray. It includes *Diplacanthus striatus, D. tenuistriatus, Rhadinacanthus longispinus, Mesacanthus pusillus, Cheiracanthus murchisoni, C. latus, Pterichthys milleri, P. productus, P. oblongus, Dipterus valenciennesi, Coccosteus decipiens, Homosteus milleri, Glyptolepis leptopterus, Gyroptychius microlepidotus, Gyroptychius [Diplopterus] agassizi, Osteolepis macrolepidotus, Cheirolepis trailli.* There appears to be no representative of the higher horizons found in Caithness and Orkney.

Among the fossil flora the most interesting is *Palaeopitys milleri*, which shows primary wood surrounded by secondary wood with medullary rays. Other plant remains include *Thursophyton milleri, Protopteridium thomsoni,* and *P. primatum.*

An interesting peculiarity of this group in the east of the Black Isle is the occurrence of pebbles of andesite and porphyritic basalt scattered through the

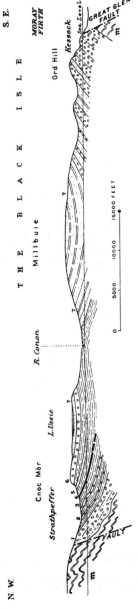

FIG. 22. *Section from Strathpeffer to the Black Isle.*

m, Moine Schists; 1-7 Middle Old Red Sandstone; 1, Basement conglomerates and sandstones; 2, Olive shales and fetid calcareous bands; 3, Fetid bituminous calcareous shales (Spa Beds); 4, Olive shales and fetid limestones; 5, Red shales passing up into sandstones; 6, Knock Farril conglomerate; 7, Red sandstones and shales.

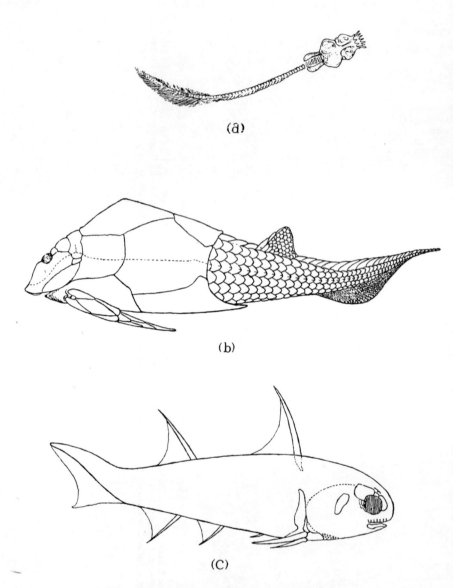

FIG. 23. *Middle Old Red Sandstone fishes.*

(a) *Palaeospondylus gunni,* length about 1 in. (after Traquair); (b) *Pterichthys milleri,* length 8 in; (c) *Diplacanthus striatus,* length 3½ in. (b and c after D. M. S. Watson).

sandstones. These igneous rocks are of the same type as the lavas of Middle
Old Red Sandstone age near Buckie on the south shore of the Moray Firth.

The large Middle Old Red Sandstone outcrop of Mealfuarvonie, south of
Glen Urquhart (Fig. 12) was mapped some years ago, but only a summary of
the results is available (Mould 1952).

Upper Old Red Sandstone

At Dunnet Head, at Dornoch, and in the area between Tain and Tarbat
Ness, strata of Upper Old Red Sandstone age appear (Figs. 19 and 21). They
consist of pink, yellow and red variegated sandstones and pebbly grits which
are strongly current-bedded and carry numerous clay-galls. Sun-cracks are
found and there is evidence of contemporaneous erosion. The sandstones of
Dunnet Head have yielded no fossils, but they are probably the Caithness

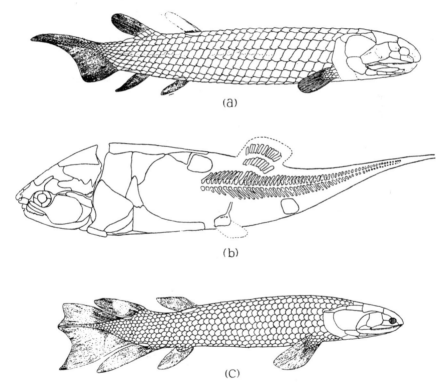

FIG. 24. *Middle Old Red Sandstone fishes.*

(a) *Thursius pholidotus*, length 12 in.; (b) *Coccosteus decipiens*, length 13 in.; (c) *Tristichopterus
alatus*, length 11 in. (restorations after D. M. S. Watson).

representatives of the yellow sandstones of Hoy which rest unconformably on
fossiliferous flagstones of the Caithness Flagstone Series. The thickness of the
Series preserved at Dunnet Head is about 2,000 ft.

Scales of *Holoptychius* have been obtained from the strata on the Dornoch
Firth. In this region the rocks are widely covered by glacial and recent deposits
and the thickness of strata present is not known.

REFERENCES

1829. SEDGWICK, A., and [Sir] R. I. MURCHISON. On the Structure and Relations of the Deposits between the Primary Rocks and the Oolitic Series in the North of Scotland. *Trans. Geol. Soc.*, 2nd Series, vol. iii, p. 125.

1834. AGASSIZ, L. On the Fossil Fishes of Scotland. *Rep. Brit. Assoc.*, p. 646.

1841. MILLER, H. *The Old Red Sandstone* (and subsequent editions).

1879. GEIKIE, Sir A. The Old Red Sandstone of Western Europe. *Trans. Roy. Soc. Edin.*, vol. xxviii, p. 345.

1888. TRAQUAIR, R. H. Notes on the Nomenclature of the Fishes of the Old Red Sandstone of Great Britain. *Geol. Mag.*, dec. iii, vol. v, p. 507.

1891. EVANS, J. W. *The Geology of the North-east of Caithness.* London.

1894-1906. TRAQUAIR, R. H. A Monograph of the Fishes of the Old Red Sandstone of Britain. Pt. II, No. 1, 1894; No. 2, 1904; No. 3, 1906, *Palaeont. Soc.*

1896. FLETT, Sir J. S. The Old Red Sandstone of the Orkneys. *Trans. Roy. Soc. Edin.*, vol. xxxix, p. 383.

1909. CARRUTHERS, R. G. On the Stratigraphical Position of the Achanarras Fauna in the Old Red Sandstone of Caithness. *Sum. Prog. Geol. Surv.* for 1908, p. 92.

1923. KIDSTON, R., and W. H. LANG. On Palaeopitys Milleri. *Trans. Roy. Soc. Edin.*, vol. liii, part ii, p. 409.

1925-1926. LANG, W. H. Contributions to the Study of the Old Red Sandstone Flora of Scotland. *Trans. Roy. Soc. Edin.*, vol. liv, pt. ii, p. 253 and pt. iii, p. 785.

1933. BAILEY, E. B., and J. WEIR. Submarine Faulting in Kimmeridgian Times: East Sutherland. *Trans. Roy. Soc. Edin.*, vol. lvii, p. 429.

1936. WESTOLL, T. S. On the Structures of the Dermal Ethmoid Shield of Osteolepis. *Geol. Mag.*, vol. lxxiii, p. 157.

1937. FORSTER-COOPER, C. The Middle Devonian Fish Fauna of Achanarras. *Trans. Roy. Soc. Edin.*, vol. lix, p. 223.

1937. WESTOLL, T. S. The Old Red Sandstone Fishes of the North of Scotland, particularly of Orkney and Shetland. *Proc. Geol. Assoc.*, vol. xlviii, p. 13.

1938. WATSON, D. M. S. On *Rhamphodopsis*, a Ptyctodont from the Middle Old Red Sandstone of Scotland. *Trans. Roy. Soc. Edin.*, vol. lix, p. 397.

1948. JARVIK, E. On the Morphology and Taxonomy of the Middle Devonian Osteolepid Fishes of Scotland. *Kungl. Svenska. Vetensk.-Akad. Handl.*, Ser. 3, vol. xxv, No. 1.

1951. WESTOLL, T. S. The Vertebrate-bearing Strata of Scotland. *Rep. of XVIIIth Internat. Geol. Congr.* (Great Brit. 1948), pt. xi, p. 15.

1952. MOULD, D. D. C. P. The Middle Old Red Sandstone of Mealfuarvonie, Inverness-shire. *Trans. Edin. Geol. Soc.*, vol. xiv, p. 422.

1956. MCINTYRE, D. B., W. L. BROWN, W. J. CLARKE and D. H. MACKENZIE. On the Conglomerates of supposed Old Red Sandstone Age near Tongue, Sutherland. *Trans. Geol. Soc. Glasgow*, vol. xxii, p. 35.

A bibliography will be found in 'The Geology of Caithness' (*Mem. Geol. Survey*), 1914. See also Geological Survey Memoirs (p. 104) on Beauly, Lower Findhorn, Ben Wyvis, Strath Oykell, Golspie, and Central Sutherland.

A.—STACKS OF DUNCANSBY, CAITHNESS

B.—'THE NEEDLE', FROM SOUTH SIDE OF ASHY GEO, CAITHNESS

A.—JURASSIC STRATA IN BEACH, FAULTED DOWN AGAINST OLD RED
SANDSTONE IN CLIFF. PORT AN RIGH, CROMARTY

B.—LATERAL AND TERMINAL MORAINES. LOCHAN AN IASGAICH, ROSS-SHIRE

X. CARBONIFEROUS

STRATA of carboniferous age occur at Inninmore Bay, on the north-east of the Sound of Mull, as a small faulted outlier. The sediments are at least 300 ft and possibly as much as 500 ft thick, and dip to the north beneath the basal breccia of the Trias. Various horizons in the sequence yield fossil plants which, though containing no diagnostic species, form an assemblage suggesting an early Coal Measures age. They have, however, yielded neither marine nor freshwater shells.

The lower part of the sequence consists mainly of white, yellow, and grey sandstones, grey and black sandy shales, and impure fireclay. Thin lenticles of coal occur but are of no economic value. The higher strata consist mainly of massive yellowish pebbly sandstone with some thin beds of lilac-coloured shale.

The fossil flora includes the following species: *Adiantites bondi, Mariopteris muricata, Neuropteris gigantea, N. heterophylla, Sphenopteris striata, Stigmaria ficoides, Annularia radiata, Asterophyllites charaeformis, A. equisetiformis, A. grandis, Calamites suckowi, C. cisti, C. schutzeiformis, C. undulatus, Cordaites principalis, Artisia approximata, Pinnularia capillacea,* and the seeds *Samaropsis* and *Carpolithus.*

W. Q. Kennedy (1946, p. 67) has suggested that the Carboniferous rocks of Inninmore and those of the Pass of Brander, 22 miles to the E.S.E. at the head of Loch Awe and lying on the other side of the Great Glen, occupy a pre-Carboniferous Valley, and that the two outcrops thus indicate a pre-Upper Carboniferous age for the main transcurrent movement along the Great Glen Fault.

REFERENCES

1934. MACGREGOR, M., and W. MANSON. The Carboniferous Rocks of Inninmore, Morvern. *Sum. Prog. Geol. Surv.* for 1933, pt. ii, p. 74.
1946. KENNEDY, W. Q. The Great Glen Fault. *Quart. Journ. Geol. Soc.,* vol. cii, p. 41.

XI. LATER MINOR INTRUSIONS

Volcanic Vents. The basal group of the Middle Old Red Sandstone of Ben Griam More, Sutherland, is cut by a plug of porphyrite and basic andesite. The rocks are of Lower Old Red Sandstone type and the intrusion may be a very late member of the 'Newer Granite' suite.

Near Dunnet Head a vent filled with slaggy basic rock pierces Upper Old Red Sandstone strata and near Duncansby Head another breaks through sandstone of the John o' Groat's group. The Duncansby vent is filled by agglomerate and dykes of nepheline-basalt. The agglomerate consists of bombs of nepheline-basalt, fragments of biotite, augite and olivine, small masses of carbonated peridotite and pieces of sandstone, limestone and gneiss. The intrusive basalt also is crowded with fragments of foreign material which is mainly sandstone but includes gneiss, granite, and quartz-porphyry. The age of all these intrusions is uncertain. Vents of similar material cut the Rousay Flags and Lower Eday Sandstone of South Ronaldshay, Orkney.

Quartz-dolerite occurs in the country west of Loch Linnhe as broad dykes and elongated bosses, often linearly arranged, which trend between E.-W. and S.E.-N.W. The intrusions cut the Strontian Granite and dykes of felsite and porphyrite, but are themselves cut by E.-W. camptonite and by N.-S. Tertiary dykes. The dykes are believed to be contemporaneous with the Permo-Carboniferous quartz dolerite/tholeiite dyke-suite of the Midland Valley and Grampian Highlands (Richey 1939; MacGregor 1948). The dykes, up to 150 ft wide, and the bosses cause intense contact-alteration at their margins.

Camptonite and Monchiquite. Dykes, mainly of monchiquite, are widespread but not numerous in northern Caithness and Sutherland. They trend E.-W. or N.E.-S.W.—that is, parallel to the dykes of camptonite in Orkney. Near Dunnet Head they traverse strata of Upper Old Red Sandstone age.

South of Loch Naver no intrusions of this character appear until along the borders of Ross-shire and Inverness-shire camptonites and monchiquites are represented by a group of dykes extending W.S.W. from the neighbourhood of Loch Monar (Ramsay 1955).

In the south-west of the region comparatively narrow dykes of camptonite and monchiquite are numerous and trend W.-E. to N.W.-S.E. None has been found to cut Mesozoic strata or Tertiary basalt lavas. Age determinations by the helium method have shown that in Colonsay north-westerly monchiquite dykes similar to those of the mainland are of late Carboniferous or Permian age (Urry and Holmes 1941). Several camptonite dykes cut quartz-dolerites in the Ardnamurchan area and, in their turn, are cut by N.-S. basalt and dolerite dykes of Tertiary types. On balance of evidence it thus seems probable that the camptonite and monchiquite dykes are of Permian age (Richey 1939; MacGregor 1948). The E.-W. camptonitic dykes in the Loch Sunart area are often crushed and are then associated with mineral veins which locally contain barytes and galena, as at the well-known lead mines of Strontian.

In the south-west of the region two small volcanic vents, related to the camptonite-monchiquite suite and containing blocks of country rock and of carbonated peridotite or of fourchite, have been described (MacGregor 1948, p. 138; Hartley and Leedal 1951). The monchiquite dykes not infrequently contain sporadic xenocrysts of hornblende and biotite and xenoliths of peridotite. The mineralogy of a narrow dyke exceptionally rich in xenoliths of peridotite and with a few of pyroxenite and country rock has been described by Walker and Ross (1954). Information on the distribution of dykes in the south-west of the region is given by Leedal (1951) and by Johnstone and Wright (1951).

Tertiary dykes are numerous from Loch Alsh southwards but are quite rare north of Loch Carron. Their trend varies between N.-S. and N.W.-S.E. Petrographically they are mainly tholeiites and olivine-dolerites.

Outer Hebrides. The younger dykes of the Outer Hebrides are mainly olivine-dolerites and crinanites belonging to the Tertiary dyke-swarms. A few quartz-dolerites and camptonites of uncertain age have been noted.

REFERENCES

1913. FLETT, Sir J. S. *In* The Geology of Central Ross-shire. *Mem. Geol. Surv.*, p. 79.
1914. FLETT, Sir J. S. *In* The Geology of Caithness. *Mem. Geol. Surv.*, p. 107.
1923-1934. JEHU, T. J., and R. M. CRAIG. Geology of the Outer Hebrides. *Trans. Roy. Soc. Edin.*, vol. liii, p. 419, and p. 615; vol. liv, p. 467; vol. lv, p. 457; vol. lvii, p. 839.
1924. BAILEY, E. B. *In* The Tertiary and post-Tertiary Geology of Mull. *Mem. Geol. Surv.*, p. 377.
1931. READ, H. H. *In* The Geology of Central Sutherland. *Mem. Geol. Surv.*, p. 197.
1939. RICHEY, J. E. The Dykes of Scotland. *Trans. Edin. Geol. Soc.*, vol. xiii, p. 393.
1941. URRY, W. D., and A. HOLMES. Age Determination of Carboniferous Basic Rocks of Shropshire and Colonsay. *Geol. Mag.*, vol. lxxviii, p. 45.
1948. MacGREGOR, A. G. Problems of Carboniferous-Permian volcanicity in Scotland. *Quart. Journ. Geol. Soc.*, vol. civ, p. 133.
1951. HARTLEY, J., and G. P. LEEDAL. A Monchiquite Vent, Stob a'Ghrianain, Inverness-shire. *Geol. Mag.*, vol. lxxxviii. p. 140.
1951. JOHNSTONE, G. S., and J. WRIGHT. The Camptonite-Monchiquite Suite of Loch Eil. *Geol. Mag.*, vol. lxxxviii, p. 148.
1951. LEEDAL, G. P. Faulted Permian Dykes in the Highlands. *Geol. Mag.*, vol. lxxxviii, p. 60.
1953-56. MacGREGOR, A. G., and others. In *Sum. Prog. Geol. Surv.* for 1951, pp. 45, 46; for 1952, p. 36; for 1953, p. 48; for 1954, p. 49; for 1955, p. 48.
1954. WALKER, G. P. L., and J. V. ROSS. A Xenolithic Monchiquite Dyke near Glenfinnan, Inverness-shire. *Geol. Mag.*, vol. xci, p. 463.
1955. MacGREGOR, A. G. Xenolithic Monchiquite. *Geol. Mag.*, vol. xcii, p. 82.
1955. RAMSAY, J. G. A Camptonitic Dyke Suite at Monar, Ross-shire and Inverness-shire. *Geol. Mag.*, vol. xcii, p. 297.

XII. MESOZOIC AND TERTIARY

IN the northern mainland of Scotland Mesozoic strata are preserved in Wester Ross, in Cromarty, and East Sutherland. The strata in Wester Ross include only Trias and Lias (Fig. 25), but on the east coast there is a broken succession from Trias to Kimmeridge in the long coastal strip between Golspie and Helmsdale (Fig. 26), and strata ranging from Estuarine Series to Kimmeridge Clay appear also on the shore at Port an Righ and Ethie, which lie respectively north and south of the mouth of the Cromarty Firth (Fig. 26, inset). Lower Cretaceous and Tertiary sediments are found at Leavad, Caithness, in a large mass glacially transported from the bed of the Moray Firth (p. 90).

Mesozoic strata are exposed at many places in Morvern and Ardnamurchan, in the south of the region. They are described along with the Mesozoic rocks of the Inner Hebrides by Dr. J. E. Richey in the volume 'Scotland: Tertiary Volcanic Districts' of this series of handbooks, and will only be briefly mentioned in the following pages.

TRIAS

Small outliers of unfossiliferous breccias, conglomerates, and sandstones resting unconformably on Torridon Sandstone are widespread along the coast of Wester Ross (Fig. 25). The largest outlier, between Sand and Aultbea, shows a lower group of breccias and conglomerates, composed of Torridonian and Cambrian materials, alternating with red, mottled, false-bedded argillaceous sandstones. This group, which is over 500 ft thick, passes up into red and variegated clays and marls with thin sandstones, amounting to 200 ft in thickness and followed by a further 200 ft of white and green arenaceous strata. At Applecross similar conglomerates and red clayey and marly beds carrying concretionary limestone, outcrop beneath Liassic strata. This position and their lithology indicate the strata as most probably of Triassic age.

At Dunrobin, East Sutherland, pale sandstones overlain by red and green marls with a band of cherty limestone above are exposed on the coast. The limestone was correlated by Judd with the 'Cherty Rock' of Stotfield near Elgin, which lies some distance above the reptiliferous sandstone and marls. Similar cherty limestone overlying an arenaceous series outcrops also in Mull and Morvern from beneath strata of Rhaetic age.

Patches of conglomerate and breccia formed of local schists and gneisses, red sandstones, marls and cornstones are widespread in Morvern, and in places the cornstones vein the schists.

The Stornoway conglomerate in Lewis may possibly be of Triassic age (p. 45).

JURASSIC

Rhaetic. At Applecross there is no recognizable development of Rhaetic, but at Dunrobin 250 ft of unfossiliferous pebbly grits and conglomerate are referred to this formation. The conglomerates contain pebbles of chert and limestone derived from the underlying Trias.

Fossiliferous sandstone possibly of Rhaetic age occurs in Morvern.

Lias. On the west coast at Applecross (Fig. 25) Lias strata, corresponding

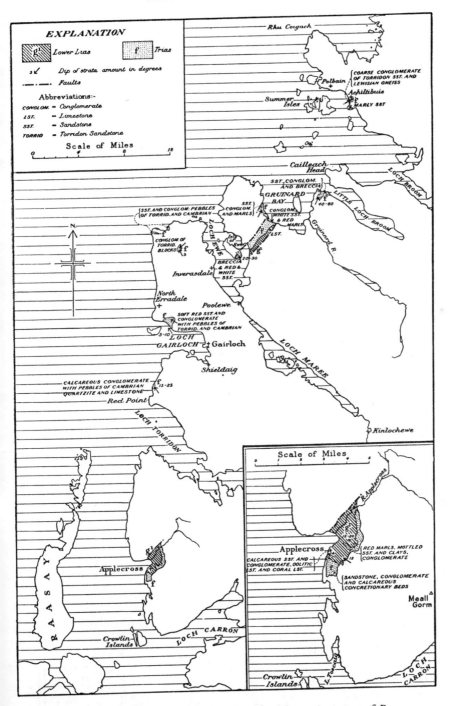

FIG. 25. *Trias and Lias of Wester Ross* (*the Mesozoic strata of Raasay,*
Scalpay and Skye are omitted).

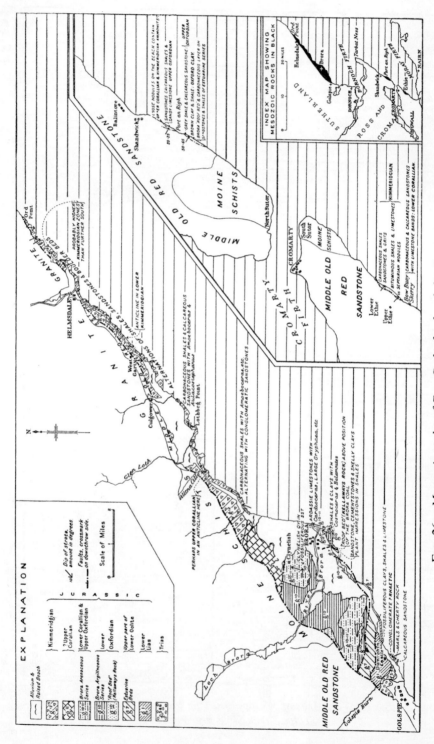

Fig. 26.   *Mesozoic rocks of East Sutherland and the Cromarty area.*

to the Broadford Beds of Skye, consist of a lower group which is predominantly limestone and an upper group of sandstones and sandy shales. The succession is 150 ft thick and represents the Hettangian stage, with possibly the lower part of the Sinemurian. The fauna includes *Thecosmilia martini, Cardinia* cf. *listeri, Modiola scalprum, Ostrea liassica, Schlotheimia* cf. *montana*. In the faulted strip between Gruinard Bay and the Isle of Ewe poorly exposed sandy limestone, blue argillaceous limestone and blue clay overlie the Trias. Numerous lamellibranch shells, indicative of Sinemurian age, have been obtained from loose blocks of limestone on the shore near Aultbea.

The Lias sediments on the east coast (Fig. 26) are much thinner and less well exposed than at Applecross. Moreover, they show a different type of sedimentation and consist of argillaceous sediments, containing thin seams of coal, overlain by sandstone, shale, and clay with two thin limestones. Only the upper beds are exposed near Dunrobin, the lower being known only from temporary exposures after heavy storms. The fauna includes the ammonites *Apoderoceras leckenbyi, Coeloceras* aff. *pettos*, ? *Echioceras rothpletzi, Prodactylioceras* aff. *davoei*, and numerous shells among which *Spiriferina pinguis, Grammatodon intermedius* and *Hippopodium ponderosum* may be mentioned. Several zones recognized in the Lower Lias of western Scotland have not been detected in the east Sutherland succession, and the decrease in thickness there may therefore be ascribed in part to non-sequence. But it has been found that species belonging to five life-zones, which are not contiguous in their type districts, occur within 13 ft of strata. In western Scotland the same interval is occupied by deposits locally reaching 700 ft in thickness. The meagre development in the east is therefore partly due to diminution of the rate of sedimentation. Domerian and Upper Lias sediments are probably cut out by a large E.-W. fault.

In the south of the region Lower Lias is exposed at many localities in Morvern and Ardnamurchan; Middle and Upper Lias are found on the mainland only near Kilchoan, Ardnamurchan.

Estuarine Series. Inferior Oolite strata are exposed in Ardnamurchan, but in eastern Sutherland the sediments of this age are cut out, along with the Upper Lias, by a fault. The strata which are exposed adjacent to the Lower Lias in this district belong to the Estuarine Series (Fig. 26). North of Dunrobin they strike E.-W., but seawards their outcrop bends sharply northwards and reaches the coast again south of Brora. The lowest strata exposed consist of massive sandstone, 50 ft thick, overlain by clays containing ribs of brecciated cementstone and sandstone. From the clays petrified wood and plant impressions have been obtained, the flora including *Equisetites beani, E. broraensis, E. columnaris, Coniopteris hymenophylloides, C. quinqueloba, Todites williamsoni, Cladophlebis denticulata, Ginkgo digitata, Dictyophyllum sp., Bucklandia milleriana, Yatesia crassa, Y. joassiana*. Higher in the succession are beds of bituminous black shale overlain by the Brora Coal, which is 3 ft 6 in thick. The black shales have yielded 'Estheria', species of *Cyrena, Perna mytiloides, Potamomya sp., Unio sp.*, and ? *Pleuromya decurtata*.

In the Cromarty area, the lowest Jurassic beds exposed belong to the Estuarine Series and outcrop at Port an Righ (Fig. 26) where clays and shales, with a band of comminuted shells including *Perna* and *Cyrena jamesoni*, overlie a thick white sandstone. The Brora Coal is represented by a 4-in carbonaceous layer above the clays.

Black fissile shales containing '*Estheria*' *murchisonae* are found at Kilchoan, Ardnamurchan.

Brora Roof-Bed: Lower Oxfordian. Above the coal at Brora there is a 3 to 5 foot hard, sandy, ferruginous limestone, and at Port an Righ in the same position a 1 to 2 foot dark, calcareous sandstone. This is the Kellaways Rock horizon and has the local name of Brora Roof-bed. The fauna is that of the *Koenigi* Zone of the base of the Yorkshire Kellaways Rock, and includes some of the type species described by J. de C. Sowerby, namely *Pholadomya murchisoni, P. acuticostata, Anatina? undulata, Protocardium striatulum,* and *Gowericeras gowerianum.* In addition the bed yields numerous shells, among which lamellibranchs are predominant. At Port an Righ the fossils of the bed are mainly lamellibranchs, and the top three inches are crowded with belemnites.

Brora Shales: Lower Oxfordian. Above the Brora Roof-bed comes a thick shaly series only fragmentarily preserved at Port an Righ but well exposed around Brora (Fig. 26), where one of the clay beds in the upper part is quarried for brick-making. The series consists of a lower group of soft black shales, 150 ft thick, containing large belemnites, lamellibranchs, and ammonites, succeeded by 125 ft of sandy and clayey shales. The latter have yielded numerous belemnites and Kosmoceratids, and contain some large septaria and fragments of lignitic wood. The *calloviensis* Zone appears to be absent at both Brora and Port an Righ, and the strata belong to the lower half of the *ornatum* Zone. The fauna consists largely of ammonites and belemnites including *Kosmoceras elizabethae, K. sedgwicki, K. stutchburi, Zugokosmoceras zugium, Belemnites oweni, B. sulcatus,* and the lamellibranchs *Grammatodon montanyensis, Lucina lirata, Pseudomonotis sp. nov., Thracia depressa, Cerithium muricata,* and *Gryphaea bilobata.*

Brora Arenaceous Series: Upper Oxfordian-Lower Corallian. The Brora Shales are succeeded by an arenaceous series in which the general sequence is as follows:

		Ft.
LOWER CORALLIAN ..	Soft sandstones, carbonaceous clays and sandy shales (thickness unknown)	—
	Limestones, alternating with carbonaceous sandstones (Ardassie Limestones)	16
UPPER OXFORDIAN ..	Sandstones, locally variegated and fossiliferous (Brora Sandstone)	100
	Sandstone with *Pteria braamburiensis*	6
	White sandstone with casts of shells	15
	White sandstone passing to quartzitic sandstone (Clynelish Sandstone)	20
	Sandstones, mostly thin-bedded and earthy, with lenticular limestones, and passing down into more shaly efflorescent beds (Fascally Sandstone) .. .. .. about	30

These strata have yielded a rich fauna. In the Fascally Sandstone ammonites include such well-known species as *Bourkelamberticeras macrum, B. lamberti,* and *Peltoceras* cf. *arduennense.* The Clynelish Sandstone provides the genotype of *Sutherlandiceras albisaxeum* in addition to species of *Aspidoceras* and numerous lamellibranchs. The sandstone itself is remarkable for its tendency to undergo silicification. When freshly quarried it is soft and easily cut, but on exposure becomes exceedingly hard and tough and therefore makes an excellent building stone. The lamellibranch *Pteria braamburiensis* is named after Braamberry Hill near Brora.

The Ardassie Limestones yield a fauna characterized chiefly by species of *Cardioceras*, such as *C. cordatum, C. excavatum, C. multonense, C. tenuicostatum* and other forms. The associated shells are mainly of lamellibranchs which include *Cucullaea pectinata, Exogyra nana, Goniomya v-scripta, Gryphaea dilatata, Lima laeviuscula, L. rigida*. The higher beds are covered by drift and raised beach in the Brora district but are represented in the Cromarty area.

At Port an Righ and southwards at Cadh' an Righ about 140 ft of strata visible at low water belong to the Brora Arenaceous Series, but differ in being more calcareous. They contain representatives of the Horton and Studley beds of the Upper Oxfordian which have not yet been found at Brora; on the other hand, the characteristic *Sutherlandiceras* fauna of the Clynelish Sandstone is absent for some reason as yet not determined. The lowest beds of the series belong to the *Lamberti* Zone and were correlated by S. S. Buckman with the Fascally Sandstone. The higher beds at Port an Righ mainly belong to the Lower Corallian, and the highest, a dark sandstone rather poor in fossils, was correlated by Buckman with the Headington Beds of the Corallian Limestones at Oxford.

At Bow Buoy Skerry, south of Ethie (Fig. 26), lenticular bands of limestone in carbonaceous sandstone have yielded ammonites characteristic of the Horton and Studley beds of Oxfordshire—for example, *Cardioceras costellatum, C.* aff. *costicordia, C.* aff. *cardia*.

Upper Corallian and Kimmeridgian. Strata of this age outcrop along the coast from Kintradwell to Dun Glas on the border of Caithness, and in a narrow strip at Ethie, south of Cromarty, where they are visible only at low tide. Their presence below low water at Port an Righ is indicated by the occurrence of loose nodules on the beach which contain *Amoeboceras (Priodonoceras) serratum, A.(P.) mansoni*, and *Pictonia* cf. *parva*. The strata at Ethie belong mainly to the *Rasenia cymodoce* Zone and yield the zonal form together with *R. uralensis* and *Amoeboceras kitchini*. The beds include carbonaceous shales, sandstones and grits, bituminous shale, limestones, and septarian nodules of brittle blue limestone; the total thickness is small.

In a recent paper the Ethie strata have been referred by C. D. Waterston (1951) to the three Eo-Kimmeridgian zones proposed by Spath, and he has drawn attention to the mixed Boreal-Mediterranean character of their macrofauna of lamellibranchs and cephalopods and also to the richness of their microfauna. In another paper Waterston (1950) re-opens the question of the origin of the well-known sandstone 'sills' and 'dykes' at Ethie and puts forward the view that they are due to intrusion, from below, of sand and water into fissures of seismic origin.

In Sutherland the Kimmeridge strata were divided by G. W. Lee into two lithological groups. The lower, known as the Allt na Cuile Sandstones, consists of 100 ft of massive unfossiliferous sandstone overlain by about 100 ft of alternating sandstone and soft carbonaceous shales. This group was originally regarded by H. B. Woodward as Upper Corallian, and lately J. Pringle also has adopted this view.

Lee's higher group consists of an alternating series of carbonaceous sandy and clayey shales, flaggy sandstones, thin grits, and boulder beds. The latter are generally about 5 or 6 ft thick but may be much thicker. Bailey and Weir

7

state that the boulder bed at Dun Glas is over 200 ft thick. These remarkable beds consist of immense angular blocks and smaller waterworn stones of Middle Old Red Sandstone rocks embedded in a matrix of gritty shelly limestone. Thus Old Red fishes are obtained from the blocks, while the matrix yields Jurassic plants and a fauna of a littoral marine type, including *Rhynchonella sutherlandi*, one of the largest of Mesozoic brachiopods and so far known only from the Kimmeridge of Sutherland. Large masses of the coral *Isastraea oblonga* are set in the matrix. These breccias or boulder beds were regarded by H. B. Woodward and M. Macgregor as the talus from cliffs and the remains of stacks of Old Red Sandstone strata which bordered the Jurassic sea. Recently Bailey and Weir have put forward the view that the breccias collected at the base of a submarine fault-scarp, the littoral shells and plant debris being swept down from the upthrow side along with debris of Old Red Sandstone by tsunamis, or tidal waves energized by earthquakes along the fault.

The shales and sandstones separating the boulder beds yield both marine fossils and plants, but the fossils do not occur in well-defined fossiliferous bands. Zones II to V, *cymodoce* to *pseudomutabilis* of Salfeld's classification, are known to be present. Kitchin and Pringle suspected the presence of the *Gravesia* Zones, and confirmatory indications of these and of the *Virgatites* Zone of Salfeld were obtained by Bailey and Weir. The thickness of the Kimmeridgian present in this area was estimated by Lee as at least 700 ft, but Bailey and Weir regard 1,500 ft as a more probable value.

From the Kimmeridge beds of Ethie and East Sutherland a rich flora and fauna have been obtained. In addition to the ammonites already mentioned there are *Amoeboceras* cf. *cricki*, *A. pingue*, *Aulacostephanus eudoxus*, and *A.* cf. *pseudomutabilis*, and among the lamellibranchs *Exogyra nana*, *E. virgula*, and *Lima concentrica*. The fossil plants include *Gleichenites boodleyi*, *Thinnfeldia rhomboidales*, *Elatides curvifolia*, *Bennettites peachianus*, *Zamites carruthersi*, and numerous other genera and species.

CRETACEOUS

No Cretaceous strata are known in place in the northern mainland of Scotland, but at Leavad, Caithness, occurs a large glacially transported mass of Lower Cretaceous sandstone measuring 240 by 150 yds and 26 ft in greatest thickness. The sandstone has disintegrated into sand but contains hard concretionary masses from which *Craspedites* and *Crioceras* have been obtained. In view of the known north-westerly direction of ice-carry it is thought that this great erratic has been removed from the sea-floor off Lybster or Dunbeath. At the lower possible estimate it is nine or ten miles distant from its source.

Upper Cretaceous strata are found in many small outliers in Morvern where they rest with marked unconformity on Jurassic, Triassic, and metamorphic rocks. Glauconitic sandstones of Cenomanian age and silicified chalk of Senonian age are present, but strata referable to the Turonian stage of the Upper Cretaceous appear to be absent.

TERTIARY

Sediments of Tertiary age are known from several small outcrops in the western Highlands and islands, but the main record of Tertiary times is preserved in the lavas and intrusions of the Inner Hebrides, which are described in the volume 'Scotland: Tertiary .Volcanic Districts' of this series of hand-books. Attention is directed once more to the Leavad erratic. Beneath the Cretaceous sandstone of which this mass is mainly composed borings proved the presence of a dark green foraminiferal clay. The assemblage of foraminifera is not diagnostic but suggests that the clay belongs to some horizon in the Crag.

REFERENCES

1827. MURCHISON, R. I. On the Coal-Field of Brora in Sutherlandshire. *Trans. Geol. Soc.* 2nd Ser., vol. ii, part ii, p. 293.
1869. MILLER, H. *Sketch Book of Popular Geology*, 3rd Edition, 1869, Appendix. Edinburgh.
1873. JUDD, J. W. The Secondary Rocks of Scotland. Firs tPaper. *Quart. Journ. Geol. Soc.*, vol. xxix, p. 98.
1878. JUDD, J. W. The Secondary Rocks of Scotland. Third Paper. The Strata of the Western Coast and Islands. *Quart. Journ. Geol. Soc.*, vol. xxxiv, p. 660.
1907. STOPES, M. C. The Flora of the Inferior Oolite of Brora, Sutherland. *Quart. Journ. Geol. Soc.*, vol. lxiii, p. 375.
1911. SEWARD, A. C. The Jurassic Flora of Sutherland. *Trans. Roy. Soc. Edin.*, vol. xlvii, p. 643.
1913. SEWARD, A. C., and N. BANCROFT. Jurassic Plants from Cromarty and Sutherland, Scotland. *Trans. Roy. Soc. Edin.*, vol. xlviii, p. 867.
1916. MACGREGOR, M. A Jurassic Shore Line. *Trans. Geol. Soc. Glasgow*, vol. xvi, pt. i, p. 75.
1920. LEE, G. W. The Mesozoic Rocks of Applecross, Raasay and North-east Skye. *Mem. Geol. Surv.*
1922-23. BUCKMAN, S. S. *Type Ammonites*. London.
1925. LEE, G. W. *In* The Geology of the Country around Golspie, Sutherlandshire. Explanation of One-inch Sheet 103. *Mem. Geol. Surv.*, p. 65.
1930. Report of the East Sutherland Field Meeting. *Proc. Geol. Assoc.*, vol. xli, p. 63.
1931. LEE, G. W., and J. PRINGLE. A Synopsis of the Mesozoic Rocks of Scotland. *Trans. Geol. Soc. Glasgow*, vol. xix, p. 158.
1933. ARKELL, W. J. *The Jurassic System in Great Britain.* Oxford.
1933. BAILEY, E. B., and J. WEIR. Submarine Faulting in Kimmeridgian Times: East Sutherland. *Trans. Roy. Soc. Edin.*, vol. lvii, p. 429.
1950. WATERSTON, C. D. Note on the Sandstone Injections of Eathie Haven, Cromarty. *Geol. Mag.*, vol. lxxxvii, p. 133.
1952. WATERSTON, C. D. The Stratigraphy and Palaeontology of the Jurassic Rocks of Eathie (Cromarty). *Trans. Roy. Soc. Edin.*, vol. lxii, p. 33.
1954. MACLENNAN, R. M. The Liassic Sequence in Morvern. *Trans. Geol. Soc. Glasgow*, vol. xxi, pt. iii, p. 447.
See also Geological Survey Memoirs (p. 104) on Ardnamurchan, Mull (pre-Tertiary), Small Isles, Glenelg.

XIII. FAULTS

THE main faults of the Northern Highlands run in N.N.E. and W.N.W. to N.W. directions, but more localized groups trend E.-W. and N.-S. Their direction has little relation to their age and it is apparent that the N.N.E. and N.W. directions have been lines of weakness in this part of the earth's crust since Archaean times, for evidence of movement along individual lines at different geological periods has been obtained. Therefore on Plate VII symbols are attached showing the latest formation or intrusive episode which they affect. Pre-Torridonian faults are omitted (*see* p. 13).

Faults affecting the thrust-belt and the Moine Schists are of great interest. In the schists they have been mapped as crush-lines as it is often impossible to determine the hade and displacement. In part at least they are wrench-faults. They trend generally W.N.W. or N.W., and N.N.E., and though movement along the north-westerly group appears to have ended first, it is probable they were produced by the same crustal stresses. The greatest of the W.N.W. group is the Loch Maree Fault, and of the N.N.E. group the Strathconon Fault. Vertical displacement is present as well as lateral, and the combination can be readily deduced in the thrust-belt where strata and thrust-planes possessing different and often opposing dips are common. Examples of such faults are the Loch Carron, Loch Maree, Traligill, and Loch More Faults. It is of interest to note that when a fault of this type affects two geological boundaries which respectively dip at higher and lower angles than the resultant displacement of the fault, the mapped displacement of the boundaries is in opposite senses. The Loch Maree Fault lies along a zone of weakness dating from pre-Torridonian times.

That the Great Glen Fault also is essentially a wrench-fault is held by Kennedy, who, identifying the Strontian Granite with the Foyers Granite, estimates the horizontal displacement as 65 miles. The main movement is later than these granites and than Middle Old Red Sandstone sediments. It is earlier, according to Kennedy, than Upper Carboniferous (p. 81). Later normal faulting along its line at Ethie and along the parallel Helmsdale and Camasunary faults affects Jurassic strata. The Great Glen Fault does not affect Tertiary rocks in Mull, yet the frequent recurrence of earthquakes shows that adjustments are still taking place along its course.

Proof of the mechanical intensity of the Great Glen dislocation has been adduced by V. A. Eyles and others, who have shown that over a distance of 40 miles between Fort William and Foyers there is a broad crush-belt along the south-eastern flank of the Glen. In the stretch between Loch Lochy and Loch Oich this belt is characterized by intense cataclasis and local mylonitization. Rocks involved in the crushing include igneous rocks of Caledonian intrusive types, Old Red Sandstone sediments, and crystalline schists (Eyles and Mac-Gregor 1952). Recent work by the Geological Survey has shown that on the north-west side of the Great Glen, between Loch Eil and Loch Arkaig, the country rock, though not severely crushed as it is on the south-east side, is considerably disturbed over a zone about one mile wide, and is traversed by numerous minor crush-lines trending between N.E.-S.W. and E.N.E.-W.S.W. Camptonite dykes in this area are later than the main crushing movement along the Great Glen fracture (Johnstone and Wright 1951).

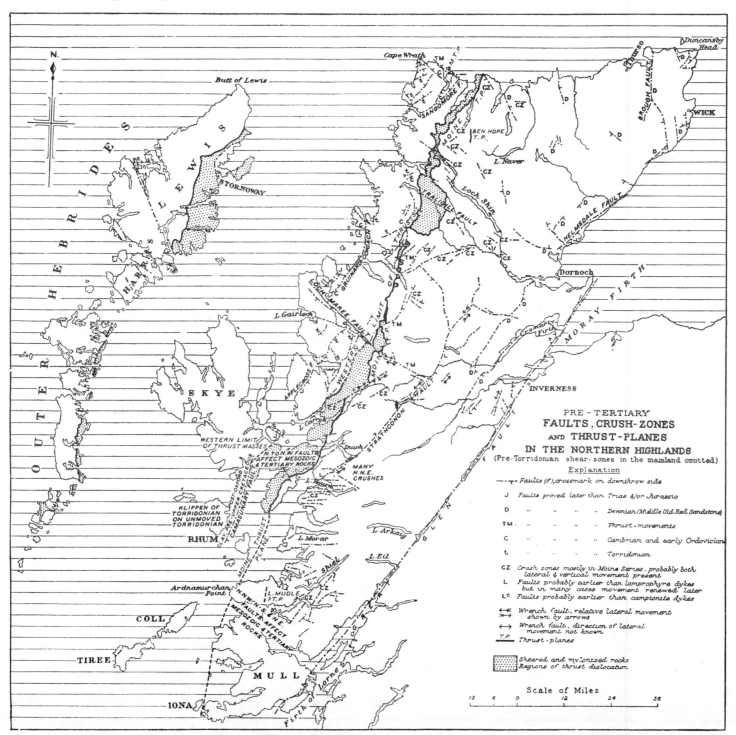

FAULT MAP OF THE NORTHERN HIGHLANDS

REFERENCES

1905. ANDERSON, E. M. The Dynamics of Faulting. *Trans. Edin. Geol. Soc.*, vol. viii, pt. iii, p. 387.
1933. BAILEY, E. B., and J. WEIR. Submarine Faulting in Kimmeridgian Times: East Sutherland. *Trans. Roy. Soc. Edin.*, vol. lvii, p. 429.
1942. ANDERSON, E. M. *The Dynamics of Faulting.* Edinburgh. (2nd Edition 1951).
1946. KENNEDY, W. Q. The Great Glen Fault. *Quart. Journ. Geol. Soc.*, vol. cii, p. 41.
1948. KENNEDY, W. Q. On the Significance of Thermal Structure in the Scottish Highlands. *Geol. Mag.*, vol. lxxxv, p. 229.
1949. ROBINSON, A. H. W. Deep Clefts in the Inner Sound of Raasay. *Scot. Geogr. Mag.*, vol. lxv, p. 20.
1951. DOLLAR, A. J. T. Catalogue of Scottish Earthquakes. 1916-1949. *Trans. Geol. Soc. Glasgow*, vol. xxi, pt. ii, p. 283.
1951. JOHNSTONE, G. S., and J. E. WRIGHT. The Camptonite-Monchiquite Suite of Loch Eil. *Geol. Mag.*, vol. lxxxviii, p. 148.
1951. LEEDAL, G. P. Faulted Permian Dykes in the Highlands. *Geol. Mag.*, vol. lxxxviii, p. 60.
1951. SHAND, S. J. Mylonite, Slickensides and the Great Glen Fault. *Geol. Mag.*, vol. lxxxviii, p. 423.
1952. EYLES, V. A., and A. G. MACGREGOR. The Great Glen Crush-belt. *Geol. Mag.*, vol. lxxxix, p. 426.
1953-54. MACGREGOR, A. G., and others. In *Sum. Prog. Geol. Surv.* for 1951, p. 46; for 1952, p. 36; for 1953, p. 48.
      See also Geological Survey Memoirs (pp. 103,104).

XIV. PLEISTOCENE AND RECENT

GLACIAL PERIOD

Two periods in the Glacial history of the Northern Highlands are recognized. In the earlier—the period of maximum glaciation—ice covered all the land and ice-movement was largely independent of topography. The length of this period is unknown. The later period, during which the ice-sheet waned and finally disappeared, is divisible into two stages: (i) the stage of confluent glaciers, when ice-streams radiating from many independent centres coalesced into great sheets which swept over the less elevated ground; and (ii) the stage of valley and corrie glaciers.

Maximum Glaciation. It is generally supposed that the ice-cap covered the highest summits of the mainland and its thickness has been estimated as at least 3,500 ft in the Loch Maree hollow. Gunn suggested, however, that An Teallach (3,483 ft) rose above the ice-cap and Clough found no sign of glaciation on Ladhar Bheinn (3,343 ft). In the Outer Hebrides the highest summits of North Harris, for example Clisham (2,622 ft), stood out as nunataks and the surface of the ice-cap rose, according to Jehu and Craig, to a height of 2,000 ft.

The position of the ice-shed on the mainland probably lay some distance east of the present watershed. A conjectural position, based on the westward carry of erratics of augen-gneiss, is shown on the sketch-map, Fig. 27. The glacial stream-lines shown have been constructed by plotting the high-level striae shown on the 1-in geological maps. It is apparent that a single general glaciation cannot account for the diversity of direction shown by these striae. In two regions particularly they point to two episodes of ice-movement on a grand scale. Caithness was traversed by ice from south-east to north-west and again from south to north. The evidence of cross-striae indicates the northerly movement as the more recent. In western Ross-shire two sets of striae, one swinging between north-west and north, the other directed generally west to west-north-west, are common at heights between 1,000 and 2,000 ft, and both occur up to 2,700 ft.

The north-westerly movement in Caithness has long been known and with it is associated a ground-moraine of stiff blue shelly boulder clay which contains, in addition to local rocks, gneisses from Ross-shire and Mesozoic rocks and fossils. The most remarkable erratic carried in this ground-moraine is the enormous mass of Lower Cretaceous sandstone and Tertiary clay at Leavad, three miles south of Spital (*see* p. 90). On Fig. 27 the western limit of the known occurrence of the shelly boulder clay in Caithness is shown by a broken line. The north-westerly movement and the shelly boulder clay are explained on the hypothesis that the eastward movement of the Scottish ice was diverted north-west by the presence across the Moray Firth of a barrier formed by the moving front of, or by ice-congestion in front of, the Scandinavian ice-sheet. The presence of striae directed almost due west at Dunnet Head suggests that the barrier lay, as shown on Fig. 27, close on the Caithness coast.

The later northerly ice-movement across Caithness must also have brought with it a shelly ground-moraine very similar to the earlier, but two shelly

94

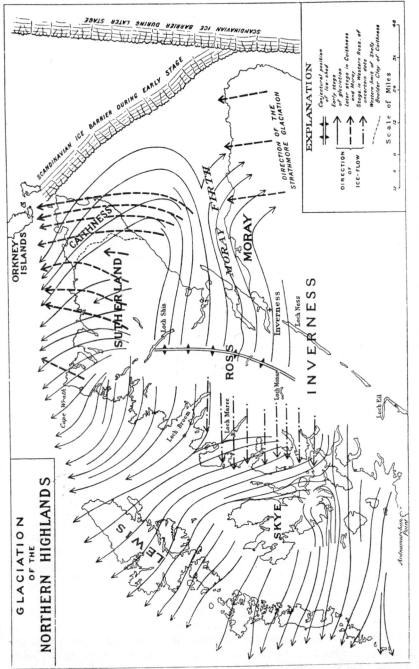

Fig. 27. *Glaciation of the Northern Highlands.*

boulder-clays have not been distinguished. During this ice-movement the barrier across the Moray Firth must have retreated eastward at least as far as indicated in Fig. 27. It appears probable to the writer that the northerly movement over Caithness was contemporaneous with the 'Strathmore glaciation' of the Grampian Highlands (see H. H. Read, 'The Grampian Highlands', British Regional Geology, p. 75 of first edition, p. 77 of second edition).

Attention may be drawn also to the existence of an early local ground-moraine beneath the shelly boulder clay.

In Western Ross-shire there is no information bearing on the relative ages of the westerly and north-westerly glaciations. The well-recognized general glaciation of north-west Scotland is that which streamed westward out over the Minch and over-rode the Outer Hebrides. During this period Skye possessed an independent ice-cap from which the pressure was sufficiently powerful to deflect the westward Scottish flow from the Loch Alsh region north-west and north along the Inner Sound of Raasay. North of Loch Ewe and south of Loch Alsh the ice on the mainland streamed steadily westward. Near Cape Wrath and along the northern coast the constant westward component of the flow (Fig. 27) suggests that this period of glaciation in the west was contemporaneous with the north-west glaciation of Caithness. In the Outer Hebrides the general direction of ice-movement is west-north-west to north-west, but westerly striae are also fairly common.

The ground-moraine of the great ice-cap has been definitely recognized on the mainland only in Caithness. Elsewhere, though boulder clay is fairly common in the lower stretches of the valleys and on smooth lower parts of the plateaux, it cannot be assigned definitely to the general glaciation, since it may equally well have been deposited during the early stages of confluent glaciation. In the Outer Hebrides the effects of glaciation are marked by erosion rather than by deposition. Here the drift is thin and rubbly and occurs in any quantity only on the west and north-west slopes of the hills. Erratics also are remarkably few and consist only of grits and quartzites referred to the Torridonian and Cambrian of the mainland. No erratics of the Tertiary basalt lavas nor of the plutonic rocks of Skye have been reported. These peculiar features of the Outer Hebridean glaciation have been explained by J. Geikie on the hypothesis that only the higher, clean strata of the ice-sheet over-rode the islands while the lower strata carrying the ground-moraine passed north and south as undercurrents along the deep channel which lies off the eastern coast.

Only in northern Lewis did the lower strata surmount the land. Here two shelly boulder clays separated by an Interglacial Bed were described by James Geikie and R. Etheridge. These have been re-studied by D. F. Baden-Powell. He records new fossils collected from a lower boulder clay, an Interglacial marine bed, an upper boulder clay and an overlying Glacial marine bed, and refers the fauna to the Pleistocene.

L. R. Wager (1953), in bringing forward evidence of local valley glaciation in St. Kilda, has confirmed the view that the ice-sheet which crossed the Outer Hebrides, 50 miles to the east, did not reach St. Kilda. He suggests that the outer edge of the main Quaternary ice-sheet lay somewhere between St. Kilda and Lewis. There is rather doubtful evidence that mainland ice may have carried boulders of Torridonian sandstone to the Flannan Isles 20 miles N.W. of Lewis, and to Sula Sgeir and North Rona about 50 miles N.W. of Cape Wrath (Dougal 1928; Stewart 1932, 1933).

A.—POST-GLACIAL GORGE IN MIDDLE OLD RED SANDSTONE CONGLOMERATE.
RIVER BEAULY AT KILMORACK

B.—RAISED BEACHES. 100-FT BEACH AND CLIFF AND PLATFORM OF
25-FT BEACH. HILTON OF CADBOLL, ROSS-SHIRE

Stage of Confluent Glaciation. This stage marked the beginning of the final dissolution of the great ice-cap. The land on the whole was still covered by ice but there was no single ice-shed. Glaciers radiated out from several well-defined centres, of which the four most important at present recognized were situated at Loch Monar, the Fannich Mountains, Ben More Assynt, and the Reay Forest.

The details of the confluent glaciation are too complex for brief description, but attention is directed to certain characteristic features of this stage. Many of the high summits stood out above the general ice-surface both within the centres of dispersion and as nunataks breaking through the ice-floods. Some of the nunataks were sufficiently extensive to act as barriers against which the ice-flow was divided; for example, An Teallach and Ben Wyvis respectively split the west and east movements from the Fannich centre. Terraced lateral moraines were deposited along the sides of nunataks and sometimes completely around them. In Glen Carron, for example, morainic terraces encircle Meall an Fhliuchard (1,330 ft) from top to bottom. During this stage great ice-lobes were pushed up into valleys which possessed no glacier of their own. These lobes have left terminal moraines in the cols at the heads of the valleys and have deposited lateral moraines whose levels rise towards the valley mouth. Moraines which cross the watersheds are clear signs of the passage of the confluent glaciers.

It is probable that the ice during this stage was effective in over-deepening the floors and straightening the sides of the larger valleys while the tributary valleys and glens were protected from erosion. Many hanging valleys can therefore be attributed to the confluent glaciation.

Valley Glacier Stage. As the accumulation of ice diminished the major valleys exercised greater and greater influence on the direction of flow and in time the glaciers were entirely restricted to the valleys and the tributary glens. They were still powerful agents of erosion and deposition and have left low-level striae which are parallel to and change direction with the valley sides. The processes of over-deepening valley floors and truncating spurs were still in operation. Probably the ground-moraine deposited in the valleys during the general glaciation was by this time largely removed, since it is usual to find bare rock outcropping along the valley sides between the hummocky lateral morainic drift of the valley-glaciers and the earlier smooth drift on the plateaux. The most conspicuous and often spectacular traces of the valley glaciers are the terminal and lateral moraines which are found in every Highland glen and strath (Plate VIb). Stages of halt in the retreat of the valley-glaciers are shown both by stepped levels of the lateral moraines and by terminal moraine barriers at intervals along the course of the valleys.

The valley glaciers were contemporaneous with the formation of the 100-foot Beach. This has been proved in two ways. In many districts the 100-foot Beach deposits merge into, and are even perhaps concealed beneath, fluvioglacial sands and gravels carried by the melt-waters from the valley-glaciers. Along many of the sea-lochs and firths—for example, Loch Hourn, Loch Duich, and the Kyle of Sutherland—no terrace of the 100-foot Beach is found even in protected positions and notwithstanding the existence of the terrace along adjacent smaller valleys. This anomaly is evidence that at the time of formation of the 100-foot Beach the main valleys were still occupied by glaciers which in some cases protruded far out into the sea-lochs of the period. Valley glaciers were still active in 50-foot Beach times.

During the latter part of the stage of confluent glaciation and throughout the valley-glacier stage erosion of corries was active. These deep recesses were probably occupied to a very late period by small corrie-glaciers which represent the final stage of active ice.

Retreat Phenomena. During the disappearance of the valley glaciers there was much deposition and erosion by melt-waters. Spreads of fluvioglacial gravel, sand, and silt were accumulated in temporary lakes held up by barriers of ice and in many cases were subsequently eroded into a series of terraces as the level of the barrier was intermittently lowered. The lakes held up against moraine barriers were smaller and are now represented by the alluvial flats which occur at intervals in every strath.

Perhaps the great ridges of sand and gravel such as the Dornoch Kame and the ridges of Tomnahurich and Torvaine, Inverness, are also to be referred to this period.

The cutting of the post-glacial river gorges (Plate VIIIa) was probably begun during the time of the temporary lakes.

The late glacial history of the Highlands is the subject of a monograph by J. K. Charlesworth (1956). In this work he considers the successive phases of the retreat of the ice since the stage of maximum glaciation, dealing individually with each main valley. In more general chapters he discusses the pattern of recession, the snow-line and methods of determining it, and correlation of stages of retreat; he then outlines the story of retreat, readvance about 100-foot Beach times and subsequent withdrawal with intermittent halt and local advance until disappearance of all but corrie glaciers.

RAISED BEACHES

Former sea-margins and beach deposits are found at levels of 100 ft, 50 ft, 25 ft, and 15 ft round the coast of Northern Scotland except in Caithness where only the lowest is present. To account for the absence of the higher beaches in this county theories involving differential depression of the land or the presence of ice, perhaps of Scandinavian origin, along the Caithness coast have been put forward, but the problem is not yet solved.

100-foot Beach. Cliffs on the north shore of the Beauly Firth (Plate VIIIb) and terraces at Brora and Helmsdale at a height of 75 to 90 ft exemplify this ancient sea-level.

In many places where trace of this beach might be expected, none exists since during the 100-foot submergence glaciers still reached the sea in some of the valleys (*see* p. 97).

The materials of the 100-foot beach are mainly sand and gravel, but in the Black Isle this beach is formed of clay and silt.

50-foot Beach. After the 100-foot submergence the land rose gradually and when the sea stood at about 50 ft above its present level relatively to the land there appears to have occurred a sufficiently long halt to permit accumulation of beach deposits. That even at this time glacial activity had not ceased is shown by the existence of moraines on top of this beach in Glen Thraill at the head of Loch Torridon. The Morar glacier extended south-south-eastwards beyond the present outlet of the loch and is believed to have provided the material for the formation of the extensive deposits of the 50-foot beach which cover the seawards continuation of the pre-glacial Morar valley. In the east of Scotland, C. H. Dinham points out the difficulty of interpreting the terraces at the 50-foot level in Lower Strath Oykell as beach deposits or as fluvioglacial outwash fans, and W. B. Wright 'is in considerable doubt as to whether the terraces ascribed to the 50-foot beach in this inner area (the upper part of the sea lochs) are raised beaches at all' (1928, p. 102).

Submerged Peat. Emergence of the land continued until the sea-level stood lower on the land than it does to-day. The interval of time which elapsed before re-submergence was sufficiently prolonged to permit the growth of forests and their later destruction by the spread of peat mosses. Remains of these early forests and peat mosses are now found beneath high-water mark at Golspie and Wick Harbour.

25-foot or Early Neolithic Beach. Submergence once more took place till the sea-margin stood near the present 25-foot contour mark, and deposits dating from this time form the 25-foot shelf which is specially extensive round the mouth of the Dornoch Firth. The beach material is composed of greenish and bluish clays, sandy clay, and sand, and carries a littoral marine fauna like that of the present day.

On the west coast, in Morar, the gravels of the post-Glacial beach rest on a wide rock-platform, at approximately 20 ft O.D., which is backed by old sea-cliffs.

In Easter Ross and Sutherland there exists at a level of 15 ft a distinct later shelf. This may perhaps be correlated with the beaches and rock platforms at heights of 8 and 5 ft in Caithness.

There are no raised beaches in the Outer Hebrides except possibly in the north of Lewis (Baden-Powell 1938). Elsewhere the evidence at present available goes to show that submergence without re-emergence has been operative since the disappearance of the ice-sheet. Along the coast peat, in which tree trunks and roots sometimes are embedded, is common below high-water mark.

CAVE DEPOSITS

At the foot of a crag of limestone, 3 miles S.S.E. of Inchnadamff, Assynt, three caves have recently been excavated. The results have not yet been published, but a preliminary investigation in 1889 by Peach and Horne provided the following record from one of the caves:

MATERIAL	LIFE, ETC.
6. Surface—peaty layer	Excrement of modern sheep.
5. Whitish marl	Land snails.
4. Red clay or cave-earth	Northern Lynx, Reindeer, Red-deer, Otter, Frog and Toad,? Arctic Lemming and Rat Vole. Fireplaces and firestones, split and burnt bones.
3. Grey clay with quartzite boulders	——
2. Bed of limestone splinters	Arctic Lemming, Field Vole, Rat Vole, Bear (?Brown), Ptarmigan, Red-grouse, Ducks, Little Auk, Puffin.
1. Gravel	——

It is probable that beds 1 to 3 were deposited while the district was sufficiently ice-bound for glaciers to occupy the valley on the side of which the cave (1,000 ft above sea-level) is situated.

REFERENCES

(See also References on p. 4)

1848. CHAMBERS, R. *Ancient Sea-Margins.* Edinburgh.
1866. JAMIESON, T. E. The Glacial Phenomena of Caithness. *Quart. Journ. Geol. Soc.*, vol. xxii, p. 261.
1870. CROLL, J. The Boulder Clay of Caithness. *Geol. Mag.*, vol. vii, pp. 209, 271.
1873. GEIKIE, J. The Glacial Phenomena of the Long Island or Outer Hebrides. *Quart. Journ. Geol. Soc.*, vol. xxix, p. 534, vol. xxxiv, 1878, p. 820.
1874. GEIKIE, J. *The Great Ice Age.* London. (3rd Edition 1894).
1879-1880. SYMINGTON GRIEVE. Preliminary Note on the Discovery of a Bone Cave at the Island of Colonsay. *Proc. Soc. Ant. Scot.*, p. 318; *and* On the Crystal Spring Cavern, Colonsay (second communication), *ibid.*, 1882-1883, p. 351.
1881. PEACH, B. N., and J. HORNE. The Glaciation of Caithness. *Proc. Roy. Phys. Soc. Edin.*, vol. vi, p. 316.
1892. PEACH, B. N., and J. HORNE. The Ice-Shed in the North-west Highlands. *Rep. Brit. Assoc.*, p. 720.
1892. HINXMAN, L. W. The Occurrence of Moraines later than the 50-foot Beach of the North-west Highlands. *Trans. Geol. Soc. Edin.*, vol. vi, p. 249.
1907. HINXMAN, L. W. The Rivers of Scotland: The Beauly and Conon. *Scot. Geogr. Mag.*, vol. xiii, p. 192.
1914. OGILVIE, A. G. The Physical Geography of the Entrance to the Inverness Firth. *Scot. Geogr. Mag.*, vol. xxx, p. 21.
1914. WRIGHT, W. B. *The Quaternary Ice Age.* London. (2nd Edition 1937).
1917. PEACH, B. N., and J. HORNE. The Bone-Cave in the Valley of Allt nan Uamh, near Inchnadamff, Assynt, Sutherlandshire. With Notes on the Bones found in the Cave, by E. T. Newton, *Proc. Roy. Soc. Edin.*, vol. xxxvii, p. 327.
1924-1934. JEHU, T. J., and R. M. CRAIG. Geology of the Outer Hebrides. *Trans. Roy. Soc. Edin.*, vol. liii, p. 419; vol. liii, p. 615; vol. liv, p. 467; vol. lv, p 457; vol. lvii, p. 839.
1928. DOUGAL, J. WILSON. Observations on the Geology of Lewis. *Trans. Edin. Geol. Soc.*, vol. xii, pt. i, p. 12.
1928. WRIGHT, W. B. The Raised Beaches of the British Isles. *Internat. Geogr. Union. First Report of the Commission on Pliocene and Pleistocene Terraces*, p. 99.
1932. STEWART, M. Notes on the Geology of North Rona. *Geol. Mag.*, vol. lxix, p. 179.
1933. STEWART, M. Notes on the Geology of Sula Sgeir and the Flannan Islands. *Geol. Mag.*, vol. lxx, p. 110.
1938. BADEN-POWELL, D. F. W. On the Glacial and Inter-glacial Marine beds of Northern Lewis. *Geol. Mag.*, vol. lxxv, p. 395.
1946. LACAILLE, A. D. The northward March of Palaeolithic Man in Britain. *Proc. Geol. Assoc.*, vol. lvii, p. 57.
1950. LACAILLE, A. D. The Chronology of the Deglaciation of Scotland. *Proc. Geol. Assoc.*, vol. lxi, p. 121.
1953. WAGER, L. R. The Extent of Glaciation in the Island of St. Kilda. *Geol. Mag.*, vol. xc, p. 177.
1954. LACAILLE, A. D. *The Stone Age in Scotland.* London.
1956. CHARLESWORTH, J. K. The Later-Glacial History of the Highlands and Islands of Scotland. *Trans. Roy. Soc. Edin.*, vol. lxii, p. 769.
See also Geological Survey Memoirs (pp. 103,104).

XV. MINERALS, ETC.

Metallic Ores. In the Northern Highlands metallic ores have been worked extensively only at Strontian in Argyllshire (p. 82), where veins containing galena associated with zinc-blende were once mined—mainly between 1722 and 1872. Lead and zinc minerals are there associated with barytes, calcite, and some strontianite, a carbonate mineral from which the element strontium was first derived. Lead and zinc ores were once worked on a small scale at Lurga in Morvern, at Struy in Strath Glass, and at Achanarras near Halkirk in Caithness. Copper ores, including bornite, malachite, and brochantite were worked to some extent about the beginning of the 19th century in a vein in Cambrian limestone at Rassal, Kishorn, Ross-shire. About 1760 an attempt was made to mine copper ore in a vein in Old Red Sandstone at Castle of Old Wick in Caithness. In 1904-5, in Lewisian Gneiss near Dornie, Loch Duich, trials were made on a band of rock rich in pyrites and pyrrhotite and containing traces of gold. Alluvial gold was worked in the Kinbrace district of Sutherland (Sheet 109) in 1869 and 1870; an unofficial estimate of the value of the metal won was £12,000. Bands of magnetite are known in the Lewisian Gneiss of Iona and Tiree; in the latter island the occurrence has been extensively investigated in recent years, but no exploitation has resulted. Vein-haematite was worked from 1870 to 1873 near Reay in Caithness, and unsuccessful trials on haematite veins near the head of Loch Kishorn were made in 1913 and 1914. Cassiterite (tinstone), distributed irregularly in magnetite-rich bands in granitic gneiss, has long been known near Càrn Chuinneag in Ross-shire.

Non-Metallic Minerals. Pegmatite veins in the Lewisian of South Harris were worked during the last war as a source of emergency supplies of potash feldspar for ceramic purposes. Other pegmatite veins, in Moine Schists at Loch Nevis, Carn Gorm, Little Scatwell, and Braetollie in Ross-shire provded small wartime supplies of white mica for electrical insulation purposes. The Loch Nevis pegmatite body contains large crystals of beryl. Barytes occurs with galena at Strontian, Lurga, and Halkirk and was worked in a vein in Old Red Sandstone near Lybster in Caithness from 1915 to 1918. A vein of graphite was once worked in the Moine Schists in Glen Strathfarrar. Thin veins of albertite traverse schists and Old Red conglomerate near Dingwall. Bands of bituminous shale are known locally in the Old Red Sandstone of Caithness.

Rocks of Actual or Potential Economic Value. During the last war olivine-rich rocks of the Lewisian of Harris were tried out for basic refractory purposes, but were not found to be of sufficient purity. Talc-rock associated with Lewisian Gneiss was mined for a few years (1931-33) at Ardintoul, Loch Alsh. Dolomite occurs in bulk around Durness and Eriboll in north Sutherland, in Assynt and in Skye; in the two latter areas it is associated with brucite-marble. These deposits have been extensively investigated of recent years in relation to possible use in the steel-making industry, and in the production of magnesium metal, but no exploitation has so far resulted. For agricultural purposes, dolomite is quarried at the present time at Ullapool, and shell sand is worked at John o' Groat's. Quartzite of high purity is available in bulk in Cambrian strata from Eriboll south-westwards to Skye; at present it is quarried only in Skye.

A sandstone of Cretaceous age, at Lochaline, Morvern, was worked during the last war as a source of silica sand for high-grade optical and other purposes; mining still continues. Jurassic coal is mined at Brora in Sutherland for local industrial use.

Constructional Materials. Before the 1914-18 war local rocks were used extensively for building purposes; at one time the Ross of Mull granite was exported to England and America. At the present day the North of Scotland Hydro-Electric Board encourages the renewed use of local stone for its building and civil engineering work (e.g. Moine psammitic granulite; Caledonian granite and Middle Old Red Sandstone). Jurassic clay (Oxford Clay) is used for brick-making at Brora. Rocks used as road metal include Lewisian gneiss, Moine psammitic granulite, and granite. Fluvio-glacial sand and gravel, and to a lesser extent morainic drift, are used in connection with roads, for making concrete-aggregate and for building purposes.

In the past, Lewisian marble from Iona and Tiree has been used for interior ornamental work and Cambrian marble from Skye as chips for terrazzo.

Mineral Waters. Sulphurous water springs from the fetid shales of Old Red Sandstone age at Strathpeffer, and the spa there makes use also of chalybeate springs issuing from glacial deposits and from muscovite-biotite-gneiss.

REFERENCES

1941. KNOX, J. Dolomite and Brucite-marble in the Scottish Highlands. *Geol. Surv. Wartime Pamphlet*, No. 6, Supplement No. 2.
1942. ROBERTSON, T., and others. Limestones of Scotland, Area VII. *Geol. Surv. Wartime Pamphlet*, No. 13.
1943. KENNEDY, W. Q., and T. R. M. LAWRIE. Commercial Mica in Scotland, pt. ii. *Geol. Surv. Wartime Pamphlet*, No. 34.
1945. ANDERSON, J. G. C. High Grade Silica Rocks of the Scottish Highlands and Islands. *Geol. Surv. Wartime Pamphlet*, No. 7, 2nd edition.
1945. ROBERTSON, T. Scottish Sources of Alkali Feldspar. *Geol. Surv. Wartime Pamphlet*, No. 44.
1946. EYLES, V. A., J. G. C. ANDERSON, D. G. R. BONNELL and B. BUTTERWORTH. Brick Clays of North-East Scotland. *Geol. Surv. Wartime Pamphlet*, No. 47.
1946. WILSON, G. V. Talc, other Magnesium Minerals and Chromite. *Geol. Surv. Wartime Pamphlet*, No. 9, 3rd Edition.
1948. WHITEHEAD, T. H. The Geological Regions of Scotland and their Minerals. In discussion on chemical resources and industries of Scotland. *Advanc. Sci.*, vol. v, No. 17, p. 22.
1951. WHETTON, J. T., and J. O. MYERS. Geophysical Survey of a Magnetite Deposit in the Island of Tiree. *Trans. Geol. Soc. Glasgow*, vol. xxi, p. 237.
1954. BUTLER, A. S., and others. *Dolomite in Scotland*. Scottish Council (Development and Industry).
1954. DUNHAM, K. C. Age-relations of the Epigenetic Mineral Deposits of Britain. *Trans. Geol. Soc. Glasgow*, vol. xxi, p. 395.
1954. FLETT, W. R., and others. *Talc in Scotland*. Scottish Council (Development and Industry).
1954. WHITEHEAD, T. H. In *Serpentine and Olivine-rock in Scotland*. Scottish Council (Development and Industry).
See also Geological Survey Memoirs (pp. 103,104).

GEOLOGICAL SURVEY MAPS AND MEMOIRS
RELATING TO THE NORTHERN HIGHLANDS[1]

(1) Maps

Quarter-Inch to One Mile Maps: *Colour printed.*
    Sheet 5. Sutherland, Caithness (West), Ross and Cromarty (North-west). 1934.
      ,, 6. Caithness (Central and East). 1920.

One-Inch to One Mile Maps:—
    (i) *Colour printed*; *Solid and Drift.*
    Sheet 35. Colonsay, with part of the Ross of Mull. 1911.
      ,, 42 and 50. Tiree. 1926.
      ,, 43. Staffa, Iona and Western Mull. 1925.
      ,, 44. Mull and south part of Morvern. 1925. Drift Edition, 1954.
      ,, 51. Coll, N.W. Mull, and W. Ardnamurchan. 1927.
      ,, 52. Morvern and Moidart. In preparation.
      ,, 53. Glen Tarbert, Loch Linnhe, Ben Nevis. 1921. Reprinted, 1948.
      ,, 60. Rum, Canna, Eigg, Muck, Oigh-sgeir. 1917.
      ,, 71. Glenelg, Loch Alsh and S.E. Skye. 1910. Drift Edition, 1956.
      ,, 81. Raasay, Applecross, Stromeferry. 1921. Drift Edition, 1954.
      ,, 82. Torridon, Glen Carron, Strath Bran. 1913. Solid Edition, 1957; Drift Edition, 1955.
      ,, 83. Strath Conon, Strath Farrar, Loch Ness. 1918. Drift Edition, 1954.
      ,, 84. Rosemarkie. 1923. Solid Edition, 1958; Drift Edition, 1954.
      ,, 92. Loch Fannich, Loch Maree. 1913.
      ,, 93. Strathrannoch, Carn Chuinneag, Glen Mòr. 1912.
      ,, 102. Strath Oykell, Lower Loch Shin. 1925.
      ,, 103. Dornoch, Golspie, Helmsdale. 1925. Solid Edition, 1950; Drift Edition, 1950.
      ,, 108. Central Sutherland. 1931. Reprinted, 1956.
      ,, 109. Sutherland (E. part) and Caithness (S.W. part). 1931. Reprinted, 1957.
      ,, 110. Caithness (S. part). 1914. Reprinted, 1956.
      ,, 116. Caithness (N. part). 1914. Solid Edition, 1957; Drift Edition, 1957.
    Assynt District with Vertical Section of Cambrian strata and 4 Horizontal Sections. 1923. Reprinted, 1951.

    (ii) *Hand-coloured.*
    Sheet 91. Gairloch. 1893.
      ,, 94. Cromarty. 1888.
      ,, 101. Ullapool, Elphin. 1892.
      ,, 107. Lochinver, Inchnadamff, Scourie. 1892.
      ,, 113. Cape Wrath, Rhiconich. 1886; partly revised, 1893.
      ,, 114. Durness, Tongue, Loch Loyal. 1889; partly revised, 1893.
      ,, 115. Strath Naver, Strath Halladale. 1898.

Six Inches to One Mile Maps: *with geological lines, uncoloured.*
    Sutherlandshire 5. Durness. 1892.
      ,, 71. Inchnadamff, Loch Assynt. 1891.

(2) Memoirs

(i) *District Memoirs, etc.*

Guide to the Geological Model of the Assynt Mountains. 1914.
The Geological Structure of the North-west Highlands of Scotland. 1907
The Geology of Caithness. 1914.
The Pre-Tertiary Geology of Mull, Loch Aline, and Oban. 1925.
The Mesozoic Rocks of Raasay, Applecross and North-east Skye. 1920.
Chemical Analyses of Igneous Rocks, Metamorphic Rocks and Minerals. 1931.
Classified Geological Photographs from the Collection of the Geological Survey of Great Britain. 1928.
Chemical Analyses of Igneous Rocks, Metamorphic Rocks and Minerals 1931-54. 1956.

---

[1] Stocks of Geological Survey publications were destroyed by enemy action. Those now on sale are listed in the latest edition of 'List of Geological Survey Maps' and of 'Government Publications: Geological Survey and Museum: Sectional List No. 45.'

104

Special Reports on the Mineral Resources of Great Britain:
Vol. II.—Barytes and Witherite. 1915; 3rd Edition, 1922.
Vol. V.—Potash-Feldspar, etc., 1916; 2nd Edition, 1917.
Vol. VI.—Refractory Materials: Ganister and Silica Rock, Sand for Open Hearth Steel Furnaces, Dolomite: Resources and Geology. 1918; 2nd Edition, 1920.
Vol. XI.—The Iron Ores of Scotland. 1920.
Vol. XVII.—The Lead, Zinc, Copper and Nickel Ores of Scotland. 1921.
Vol. XXIV.—Cannel Coals, Lignite and Mineral Oil in Scotland. 1922.
Vol. XXXII.—The Granites of Scotland. 1939.
Vol. XXXIII.—The Synopsis of the Mineral Resources of Scotland. 1940.
Vol. XXXIV.—Rock Wool. 1945; 2nd Edition, 1949.
Vol. XXXV.—The Limestones of Scotland. 1949.
Vol. XXXVI.—The Cambro-Ordovician Limestones and Dolomites of the Ord and Torran areas Skye, and the Kishorn area, Ross-shire. 1954.
Vol. XXXVII.—The Limestones of Scotland: Chemical Analyses and Petrography. 1956.

(ii) *Sheet Memoirs*

Sheet 35. Geology of Colonsay and Oronsay with part of the Ross of Mull. 1911.
„ 43. Geology of Staffa, Iona and Western Mull. 1925.
„ 51 and part of 52. Geology of Ardnamurchan, North-west Mull and Coll. 1930.
„ 53. Geology of Ben Nevis and Glen Coe. 1916. (*Second Edition in the press*).
„ 60. Geology of the Small Isles of Inverness-shire. 1908.
„ 71. Geology of Glenelg, Loch Alsh and South-east part of Skye. 1910.
„ 82. Geology of Central Ross-shire. 1913.
„ 83. Geology of Beauly and Inverness. 1914.
„ 84 and part of 94. Geology of the Lower Findhorn and Lower Strath Nairn, including part of the Black Isle near Fortrose. 1923.
„ 92. Geology of the Fannich Mountains. 1913.
„ 93. Geology of Ben Wyvis, Càrn Chuinneag, Inchbae and the surrounding country. 1912.
„ 102. Geology of Strath Oykell and Lower Loch Shin. 1926.
„ 103. Geology of the country round Golspie, Sutherlandshire, including a description of the Mesozoic Rocks of East Sutherland and Ross. 1925.
„ 108 and 109. Geology of Central Sutherland. 1931.

Printed in Scotland for HER MAJESTY'S STATIONERY OFFICE
by G. Cornwall & Sons Ltd., Aberdeen. Demand 02 0022 K 40